THE MILITARY-INDUSTRIAL COMPLEX

AMERICAN HISTORICAL ASSOCIATION –
SOCIETY FOR THE HISTORY OF TECHNOLOGY

Historical Perspectives on Technology, Society, and Culture

A Series Edited by Pamela O. Long and Robert C. Post

Other Titles Published:

Technology and Utopia
Howard P. Segal

*Transportation Technology and Imperialism
in the Ottoman Empire, 1800–1923*
Peter Mentzel

*Technology and Society in the Medieval Centuries:
Byzantium, Islam, and the West, 500–1300*
Pamela O. Long

Technology, Transport, and Travel in American History
Robert C. Post

*Technology Transfer and East Asian
Economic Transformation*
Rudi Volti

Technology and Society in Ming China (1368–1644)
Francesca Bray

*Technology, Society, and Culture in Late Medieval
and Renaissance Europe, 1300–1600*
Pamela O. Long

Title Forthcoming:

Nature and Technology in History
Sara B. Pritchard and Jim Williams

THE MILITARY-INDUSTRIAL COMPLEX

By Alex Roland

A Publication of the Society for the History of Technology
and the American Historical Association

ALEX ROLAND is professor of history at Duke University, where he teaches military history and the history of technology. He is a past preisdent of the Society for the History of Technology. His books include *Underwater Warfare in the Age of Sail* (1978); *Model Research: The National Advisory Committee for Aeronautics* (1985); and, with Richard Preston and Sidney Wise, *Men in Arms: A History of Warefare and Its Interrelationships with Western Society* (5th ed., 1991).

COVER ILLUSTRATION: The B-1 bomber went into production in 1986, almost thirty years after it was first proposed to President Eisenhower. Labeled the "born-again bomber" by journalist Nick Kotz, the B-1 demonstrated the sturdy resilience of the military-industrial complex in overcoming resistance to proposed weapons systems.

AHA EDITOR: Robert B. Townsend

EDITORIAL ASSISTANCE: Cecilia J. Dadian and Richard Bond

LAYOUT: Liz Towsend

© 2001 American Historical Association
ISBN: 0-87229-124-6

Published in 2001 by the American Historical Association. As publisher, the American Historical Association does not adopt official views on any field of history and does not necessarily agree or disagree with the views expressed in this book.

TABLE OF CONTENTS

HISTORICAL PERSPECTIVES ON TECHNOLOGY, SOCIETY, AND CULTURE

SERIES INTRODUCTION

Technology reflects and shapes human history. Technology and history have been integral to one another from the establishment of neolithic farming and food-storage techniques to the development of metallurgy, weaving, printing, and electronics. The role of the stirrup in the Middle Ages, gunpowder in the thirteenth century, printing in thc fifteenth, the steam engine in the eighteenth, factories in the nineteenth, and nuclear power in the twentieth—are all subjects of an expansive scholarly literature. This literature spotlights many animated controversies about choices made among competing techniques for attaining the same end—whether automobiles would be powered by steam, electricity, or internal combustion, for example.

Yet the import of technology and its mutual interactions with society and culture have often been neglected in the high school, college, and even university curriculum. When teachers unfamiliar with its rich historiography do consider technology, they all too often treat it as inert or determinate, lending their authority to the fallacy that it advances according to its own internal logic. Scholarly specialists now largely agree about what is called *social construction*: the idea that technologies succeed or fail (or emerge at all) partly because of the political strategies employed by "actors"—individuals, groups, and organizations—that have conflicting or complementary interests in particular outcomes. Most of them also agree that success or failure is contingent on inescapable physical realities, "that the human fabric depends to a large degree on the behavior of atoms," as the distinguished historian and metallurgist Cyril Stanley Smith put it. But there is no doubt that technological designs are shaped by ambient social and cultural factors, nor, indeed, that the shaping of technology is integral to the shaping of society and culture.

This booklet series, a joint venture of the Society for the History of Technology and the American Historical Association, draws on the analytical insights of scholars who address technology in social and cultural context. Some of them are concerned primarily with the relationship of technology to labor, economics, political structure, or the organization of production; sometimes their concern is with the role that technology plays in differentiating social status and the construction of gender; sometimes it is with *interpretive flexibility*—the perception that determinations about whether a technology "works" are contingent on the expectations, needs, and ideology of those who interact with it. Following from this is the understanding that technology is not intrinsically useful or even rational; capitalist ideology in particular has served to mask powerful nonutilitarian motives for technological novelty, among them kinesthetic pleasure, a sense of play, curiosity, and the exercise of ingenuity for its own sake, a phenomenon known as *technological enthusiasm*. As evidence of this, many inventions—from the mechanical clock during the Renaissance to the telephone and the automobile more recently—met only marginal needs at the outset. Needs with any substantial economic significance had to be contrived, thereby making invention the mother of necessity.

There are various definitions of technology. Sometimes it is defined as the way that "things are done or made," and this is a useful definition whenever one asks how things were done or made in a particular way in a particular context and then analyzes the implications of taking one path rather than another. Lynn White Jr., a historian who served as president of both the Society for the History of Technology and the American Historical Association, called this "the jungle of meaning." While the notion that technology marches of its own predetermined accord still has a strong hold on popular sensibilities, specialists in the interaction of technology, society, and culture now understand that it cannot do anything of the sort. Technology is not autonomous; rather, it is impelled by choices made in the context of circumstances in ambient realms, very often in the context of disputes over political power. Once chosen, however, technologies *can* exert a powerful influence on future choices. One only needs to consider the Strategic Defense Initiative, "Star Wars," which has been funded for decades not because it is actually feasible but because it provides partisans with effective political rhetoric.

Definitions of technology vary from one discipline to another. We believe that defining it as "the sum of the methods by which a social group provides itself with the material objects of their civilization" is sufficiently concrete without being too confining. It is important to specify the word *material*, for there are of course "techniques" having to do with everything from poetics to sex to bureaucratic administration. Some might go further and specify that "material" be taken to mean three-dimensional "things," and this seems satisfactory as long as one bears in mind that even an abstraction such as a computer program, or an idea for the design of a machine, or an ideology such as technocracy or scientific management is contingent upon its expression in tangible artifacts.

Prior to the twentieth century, issues that historians now frame in terms of the word *technology* were defined by the historical actors themselves in other terms. In his 1829 book titled *Elements of Technology*, the botanist Jacob Bigelow wrote that he used the term to encompass "the principles, processes, and nomenclature of the more conspicuous arts, particularly those which involve applications of science, and which may be considered useful." For some time, the word was used primarily in the context of technical education, a notable instance being the Massachusetts Institute of Technology, founded in 1861. For some time after that—and perhaps even today—it was not a term known to every culture. Technology still encompasses various actors' categories in diverse historical contexts, and that is part of the reason why contemporary scholars still define it variously. We believe that the complexity of definition, conceptual categories, and methodologies is instrumental in making the history of technology such a fruitful area of inquiry.

"Every generation writes its own history," said Carl Becker. In commissioning and editing the essays in these booklets, we have sought to have each one convey a broadly informed synthesis of the best scholarship, to outline the salient historiographical issues, and to highlight interpretive stances that seem persuasive to our own generation. We believe that the scholars represented in this series have all succeeded in integrating their inquiries with mainstream scholarship, and we trust that their booklets provide ample confirmation of this belief.

Pamela O. Long
Robert C. Post
Series Editors

INTRODUCTION

The Cold War between the United States and the Soviet Union (1948–91) fueled the rapid pace of technological change in the second half of the twentieth century. Microelectronics and earth-circling satellites came to provide virtually instantaneous communication around the world. Humans had broken the sound barrier in 1947 and went on to fly thirty times faster on their way to the moon. Medical research produced wonder drugs, swapped human organs, and inched toward a cyborg future of artificial body parts. Computers evolved from calculating machines to expert systems that could aid or replace human agents. Consumer goods delivered the symphony orchestra, the movie theater, climate control, and unprecedented levels of safety, ease, and comfort into the homes of the working class in the so-called "developed" countries. One of the hallmarks of the second half of the twentieth century was the staggering and often bewildering pace of technological change.

The coincidence of the Cold War with this acceleration of technological change begs the question of the causal relation between the two. The question takes two forms. First, to what extent did Cold War competition drive the pace of technological development? Obviously, many other factors were at work: the rise of globalism, the refinement of financial institutions and practices, the explosion of scientific knowledge, the culture of consumerism, the fecundity of free-enterprise capitalism, and the concentration of the world's capital in the developed countries, to name just a few. But the hothouse of innovation spawned by the military-industrial complex contributed as well. Second, how did military imperatives shape modern technology? Would we have had the same technologies and the same infrastructure had there been no military sponsorship? Do technologies always bear the imprint of the purposes for which they were first developed, or is technology simply an instrumental human creation to be measured by the work it does, not the work it was created for? Would modern computers work differently had the military played a lesser role in their development?

The answers to these questions revolve around patronage. Why does any technology ever get developed? Of course, technology often bubbles up from practice. People with jobs to do find new and better ways of doing them. But some technology is commissioned. Sponsors promote research and innovation to achieve their own ends. Every age has witnessed developments in the arts and sciences funded by patrons—governments, princes, merchants, or warlords. They might want better roads, better buildings, better art, more creature comforts, or better weapons. Dionysius I of Syracuse funded an arsenal in the fourth century B.C.E. and filled it with artisans gathered from around the Mediterranean. He sought revolutionary weapons to give him a military advantage over his enemies. He got the catapult.

Patronage is therefore one of the social forces that helps determine what a society produces. In Rome it was roads, aqueducts, walls, and monumental architecture. In Renaissance Italy it was art, humanism, scientific academies, the arsenal at Venice, and the *trace italienne*, a style of fortification that countered the introduction of siege artillery. In seventeenth- and eighteenth-century France it was more roads, canals, fortifications, and Versailles. In eighteenth-century England it was steam engines, factories, textile machinery, civil engineering, and Nelson's flagship *Victory*. In nineteenth-century Germany it was university research laboratories, industrial chemistry, railroads, and rifles. These developments were patronized by governments and by private interests. They served military and civil purposes; some served both.

Still, the twentieth century looks different. Perhaps it was the scale of warfare in the first half of the century, when more than 100 million people died as a direct result of war. Perhaps it was the introduction of nuclear weapons at the end of World War II, raising for the first time in human history the prospect that we might actually destroy ourselves. Perhaps it was simply an American myopia, created by the unprecedented appearance in the United States of a standing military establishment in peacetime. Whatever the cause, Americans came to believe that the military-industrial complex— the label attached to the phenomenon by President Dwight Eisenhower in his farewell address of 1961—exerted a particularly dangerous, pervasive, and pernicious influence, not just on technology but on national life in general.

These perceptions beg consideration. What role did the military play in the development of technology in the second half of the twentieth century? And did that military role shape civil society? This pamphlet will attempt to answer both questions by examining the relationship between war and technology in the United States. It will argue in part that the term "military-industrial complex" applies most cogently to three decades of American history in the middle of the Cold War, roughly 1955 to 1985. It may be used to label the relationship between any state and its arms industry, but it best describes the phenomenon that President Eisenhower warned against.

The analysis will focus on five broad relationships transformed by the military-industrial complex: (1) civil-military relations, (2) the relations between industry and the state, (3) the relations among government agencies, (4) the relations between the scientific/technical community and the state, and (5) the relationship between society and technology.[1] First, however, a brief overview of the military-industrial complex is in order.[2]

1

Defining the Complex

Two great ironies surround Dwight Eisenhower's warning about the military-industrial complex. First, Eisenhower had long been an advocate of closer cooperation between the military and industry. As a young lieutenant he had observed firsthand the painful lack of military-industrial cooperation in World War I. Already a world-class industrial power by 1917, the United States was slow to mobilize the latent power of industry to serve its war effort. The government spent over $1 billion for aircraft in World War I but only 960 planes reached the front, not a single fighter among them.[3] Similarly, the American emergency shipbuilding program of World War I spent $3 billion, paid twice as much per ship as the British, and did not deliver a single vessel until the last year of the war.[4] The "Merchants of Death" hearings in the 1930s fed a perception that American business had profited from the war without contributing proportionally.[5]

Nothing between the wars altered the military's belief that the next war would be less forgiving. World War I, the first truly "total war" in history, had been a conflict pitting the total resources of the state against those of its enemies. It had been a war of industrial production, won by the alliance that was able to field the most combatants and then provide them with the arms, equipment, food, and fuel necessary to fight in the machine age. Eisenhower understood that the next war would look the same. In a 1928 paper at the Army War College and again in a 1932 paper at the Army Industrial College, Eisenhower called for closer cooperation in peacetime between industry and the military, so that when war came they would be prepared to work in harmony.[6] The military had to communicate its needs to industry; industry had to meet those needs on short notice and under duress.[7]

Figure 1. *Long an advocate of closer ties between industry and the military, President Dwight D. Eisenhower grew alarmed by their relationship during his presidency. In his farewell address in 1961, he warned his fellow citizens about the dangers of a "military-industrial complex." The term attracted little attention at the time, but achieved great political salience during the Vietnam War. (Dwight D. Eisenhower Library)*

What, then, caused Eisenhower in 1961 to warn against the very phenomenon he had once promoted? World War II. Like its namesake, this was a war of industrial production. The United States was not only the arsenal of democracy; it was the factory, the breadbasket, the warehouse, and the delivery truck. Its total output of goods and services per capita rose 50 percent from 1939 to 1945; its national income in the same period doubled, while the net income of the rest of the world increased not at all. Furthermore, it led the world in a new arena of international competition that weighed just as heavily in the outcome of World War II. This was the first war in history in which the weapons in play at the end differed significantly from those at the beginning. Jet aircraft, guided missiles, radar, and the atomic bomb were just the most familiar of the new technologies to flow from the research laboratories of the major combatants. The quality of a nation's technological output rivaled quantity in the outcome of the war, breeding the perception among military observers that in the next war quality might actually count for more than quantity. Perhaps World War III would be won by the best weapons, not the most weapons.

This perception helped to transform the military's relation to technology. Throughout most of recorded history, commanders had resisted technological change, preferring the proven and familiar to the new and untested.[8] The introduction of gunpowder alienated whole generations of mounted knights, who foresaw an end to valor in war. Underwater warfare encountered stiff resistance from military establishments in the eighteenth and early nineteenth centuries until it proved its potential in the American Civil War.[9] As recently as World War I, the U.S. Navy had opposed new gunfire techniques, forcing reformer William Sims to take his case directly to President Theodore Roosevelt.[10] The British Army was so stodgy in World War I that Winston Churchill, as first lord of the Admiralty and later as minister of munitions, sponsored research on an armored land vehicle within the naval establishment; its code name, "tank," was designed to make the Germans think it was a water-storage vessel.

Following World War II, the military reversed this historic pattern and rushed to embrace new technology as the desideratum of modern war. In the United States, this conversion was overdetermined. World War II had demonstrated both what American scientists and engineers could do, as well as what the Germans might have done had the war dragged on. The demobilization following World War II convinced the military services that Americans would not tolerate a large, standing armed force; the services would have to match the sheer numbers of the Soviet military establishment with technology. In the same vein, automated and sophisticated weaponry promised to improve the survivability of Americans in combat, minimizing the casualties for which democracies seemed so intolerant. Finally, the services concluded from Vannevar Bush's initiative to create a postwar National Research Establishment that if they did not set the agenda for military science and technology, the scientists and engineers might.[11] The technological enthusiasm that consequently swept the American military in the 1940s and 1950s contributed greatly to Eisenhower's alarm.

The second great irony of Eisenhower's warning is semiotic. The term he introduced into popular discourse, "military-industrial complex," found a resonance out of proportion to its descriptive value or its historical accuracy. Privately, Eisenhower called the phenomenon the "delta of power." He included Congress in a triangular nexus with the armed services and industry.[12] Collaboration among these three powerful institutions pressured him relentlessly to expand the armed forces and their budgets. Particularly galling to Eisenhower was the mindless pursuit of new and often redundant weapons systems, devices through which the services contended with each other for roles and missions and laid the groundwork for increased budgets and force levels to match their new equipment.

Others have argued that Eisenhower should have included academia in the complex, for the network clearly extended its tentacles into the country's research universities.[13] But Eisenhower chose instead to issue a separate warning about "a scientific-technological elite." This language more closely approaches the probable source of Eisenhower's warning, sociologist C. Wright Mills's influential 1956 book, *The Power Elite*.[14] Mills warned against the concentration of power in the hands of corporate, military, and political leaders. Eisenhower embraced his argument, but substituted "industry" for "corporation," drawing a distinction between manufacturers on the one hand and service businesses such as banking, finance, and insurance on the other. Though Eisenhower himself was as comfortable with scientists and engineers as he was with corporate executives, he nonetheless perceived that the "technological revolution during recent decades" was forming a new locus of power in America, centered on the development of military arms and equipment.[15]

Though Eisenhower's chosen label, "military-industrial complex," had little impact at the time, it assumed a prominent place in the national debate over the Vietnam War in the late 1960s and 1970s. Imitators invoked it as Eisenhower did, pejoratively.[16] Both "military" and "industry" have complicated and ambiguous meanings deeply rooted in American history. While the country's security and well-being have depended upon its armed forces and industry, both have also been seen as potentially threatening to the country's core values. Americans inherited from their British forebears a fear of standing armies. Colonists in North America watched the motherland go through a wrenching civil war in the middle of the seventeenth century; citizens in their homeland suffered a suspension of traditional rights and privileges during the Cromwell interregnum. When it came time for the Americans to write their own constitution in the eighteenth century, they adopted the same constraints on military power that the British had invented in the Mutiny Acts of 1689. In addition to an implied preeminence of civilian over military power, the constitution provided that the army had to be funded annually by Congress. No American Cromwell could lead a new model army in the United States without annual congressional assent.

American distrust of industry arose later. In what Mark Twain called "the great barbecue," robber barons of the late nineteenth century demonstrated to Americans the dangers of unbridled free enterprise. Technological marvels such as U.S.

Steel, Standard Oil, and the great railroad systems of William H. Vanderbilt and J. P. Morgan stoked the American industrial revolution, but also provoked the Sherman Anti-Trust Act, the Populist and Progressive movements, and a popular faith in state regulation of industry. Henry Ford and Thomas Edison became the new model industrialists in America, geniuses whose economic values and entrepreneurial styles appeared to be more in tune with the democratic principles underlying American consensus. Still, the reforms of the Progressive era failed to arrest the growth of corporate power in the United States. By the time of the Eisenhower administration, Charles E. Wilson, president of General Motors and secretary of defense, could assert without embarrassment that what was good for General Motors was good for America. If the quintessential American industry could harbor such elitist views, then surely C. Wright Mills was right about the emerging "power elite." Industry, like the military, needed close scrutiny.

By lumping these two realms together under the heading of "complex," Eisenhower imposed a sinister and worrisome overtone to an already troubling association. The "military-industrial complex" smacked of conspiracy, and the "scientific-technical elite" did nothing to dispel the ominous overtones of Eisenhower's warning. Forty years after the fact, the opprobrium implied in Eisenhower's language still hangs over the relationship between war, technology, and the state.

Viewed dispassionately, the military-industrial complex was an alliance between the defense industry and the Department of Defense to shape public policy. Military goals ranged across a broad spectrum. At one end, a bureaucratic imperative drove each service to expand its roles and missions, and with them its budget; at the other end of the spectrum, the Soviet Union challenged the armed forces of the United States to protect the country and its interests abroad against nuclear and conventional threats. Industry's goals ranged from profits on the one hand to public repute on the other; defense contractors wanted to be both wealthy and reputable. Military and industrial goals converged in the Cold War task of building an arsenal equal to the perceived challenge posed by the Soviet Union.

America's military-industrial complex in the Cold War was by no means the first instance in history when war and technology found themselves in symbiosis. Richard Cowen has discerned a military-industrial complex in the iron-producing Weald region south of London in the sixteenth century.[17] Paul A. Koistinen and other scholars have found precursors of Eisenhower's military-industrial complex earlier in American history.[18] Indeed, the term in its most general sense has been imposed anachronistically on countless previous examples of collaboration between the military and industry.

But the first scholar to discern the historical taxonomy of Eisenhower's military-industrial complex was William H. McNeill. In his 1982 book *The Pursuit of Power*, McNeill construed the relationship between the British Admiralty and the arms industry in the Anglo-German naval race at the turn of the twentieth century as being analogous to the American version half a century later. Naval officers and industrialists cooperated to shape British policy. They agreed to interpret German naval expansion as a threat to British security and to persuade the British people and their representatives in Parliament that the threat required a dramatic increase in naval spending. Their campaign fueled the naval arms race and established a model for coordinated political action. The navy got more and better ships, and industry got contracts to build and equip those ships, all in the name of national security.[19]

Eisenhower's military-industrial complex differed from McNeill's and from the others discerned by recent historians in several important ways. First was its enormous scale and nearly half-century duration. Between 1948 and 1991, the United States sustained a permanent military mobilization in peacetime. No precedent existed in all of American history. From the end of the War of 1812 until well after World War II, geography and politics had combined to provide America with free security.[20] Between 1945 and 1950, however, the administration of Harry Truman (1945–53) came to conclude that the Soviet Union posed a real threat to world stability and thus to the security of the United States. Truman vowed in 1947 to contain communist expansion. His secretary of state, General George C. Marshall, offered all nations material assistance in rebuilding their economies. Early in 1950, President Truman signed National Security Council Directive 68 (NSC 68), a landmark document that essentially committed the United States to permanent military mobilization in peacetime. The subsequent transition to a permanent war footing would have been more salient in the public consciousness had it not been masked by the Korean War; the U.S. military budget shot up during the war and never returned to prewar levels. (See charts 1 and 2, pages 9 and 10.)

The importance of technology in the ensuing Cold War became manifest in the 1950s. When the Soviet Union exploded its own atomic weapon in 1949 to match the American achievement of World War II, the United States embarked on development of a thermonuclear bomb, a fusion weapon orders of magnitude more powerful than the fission bombs of Hiroshima and Nagasaki. The defining feature of these weapons, however, was not their power but their cost. Far cheaper than fission bombs in explosive power per dollar (providing "more bang for the buck," in Cold War parlance), fusion weapons allowed the superpowers to build arsenals bristling with tens of thousands of warheads, enough destructive power to eliminate each other as functioning political entities and to irradiate their neighbors throughout the northern hemisphere. The United States tested its first hydrogen bomb in 1952; the Soviets matched the feat just ten months later.

Second in importance only to the weapons themselves were the delivery systems developed to convey them. A perceived "bomber gap" of 1955 shook American confidence in the Eisenhower administration by suggesting that the Soviets had developed a fleet of bombers capable of reaching the United States in strength. More alarming still, and far more threatening in actuality, was the launch of Sputnik two years later. If the Soviet Union had the technology to place a satellite in orbit, then it could place a nuclear weapon on New York. Furthermore, while air defenses offered at least partial protection from bomber attack, no known technology could intercept an intercontinental ballistic missile (ICBM).

The Soviet Union, hitherto seen as a backward and underdeveloped society, had produced two paired technologies that left the United States defenseless to a devastating attack.

In the wake of Sputnik, public fear bordering on paranoia, already manifest in the McCarthy panic of the early 1950s, broke over the Eisenhower administration. This public response compounded the already relentless pressure on the military budget that the president had felt since inheriting the Korean War from Harry Truman. The military-industrial complex pushed public policy in the direction of more and better weapons, expansion of roles and missions, and mobilization of the civilian economy in the service of the state. The army and the air force launched parallel development programs to field intermediate-range ballistic missiles.[21] The navy and the air force raced each other to develop solid-fuel ballistic missiles, one to arm strategic submarines and the other to enhance the readiness of land-based ICBMs.[22] All the services proposed space activities to ensure for themselves a niche in this new realm of human activity. While the United States continued to fight the Cold War with diplomacy, propaganda, foreign aid, and other traditional tools of international relations, the race for new and better weapons defined the East-West struggle.

Nor did the race restrict itself to traditional military realms. In a war pitting the total resources of the state against its enemies, all agencies of government and all walks of life were subject to enlistment. Intelligence traditionally served both military and civilian purposes. President Truman created a Central Intelligence Agency in 1947 to coordinate data gathering and analysis. The services in turn enlarged their own intelligence organizations and in time created a Defense Intelligence Agency. Atomic energy found itself consigned to a succession of agencies—the Atomic Energy Commission, the Energy Research and Development Administration, and the Department of Energy—all of which struggled to keep the production of nuclear weapons from driving their agendas. In the wake of Sputnik, Eisenhower empanelled a President's Science Advisory Committee, created an Advanced Research Projects Agency, and reorganized the Department of Defense—all attempts to gain civilian control over the armed services' competitive pursuit of new technology. The president also created the National Aeronautics and Space Administration (NASA, 1958) to prevent the heavens from becoming a new military arena. He could not, however, keep NASA from fighting the Cold War by other means. Nor could he finally keep the military services from exploiting space. He squashed the army's proposal for Project Horizon, to establish a base on the moon under the precept that armies always "take the high ground."[23] But he failed to prevent the services from using space for weather forecasting, strategic targeting, communications, and, of course, intelligence. Military spending on space lagged behind civilian expenditures through the Apollo years (1961–75), but regained the lead over the last eighteen years of the twentieth century.[24]

The contest over defense spending persisted throughout the Cold War under the banner "How Much Is Enough?"[25] Could the country afford to place an economic

8

limit on its own security? Eisenhower argued strenuously that it could, indeed it must. He conceived a "great equation" that balanced military preparedness against sustainable economic growth. He expected the Cold War to be fought over "the long haul"; the winner would have to provide adequate security without bankrupting itself.[26] This calculus helps to explain the defense expenditures of the Cold War and especially the nation's investment in research and development.

Chart 1 tracks total federal spending and military spending as a percentage of gross domestic product (GDP).[27] Following World War II, both fell precipitously, only to rise again in the early 1950s in response to the Korean War and the permanent military mobilization prescribed by NSC 68. Thereafter, however, defense spending generally fell as a percentage of GDP, though it did not reach pre–Korean War levels until after the end of the Cold War. Only the Vietnam War (1965–73) and the Gulf War (1990–91) changed this pattern. All the while, total government spending was increasing as a percentage of GDP.

Chart 2, showing military spending as a percentage of government spending, tells a slightly different story. In this context, military spending returned to pre–Korean War levels in 1975, following the Vietnam War. The exceptions to the general pattern of this spending occur during the Vietnam War and again in the presidency of Ronald Reagan. In all other periods, nonmilitary programs absorbed an ever-increasing percentage of federal outlays.

Spending on research and development (R&D) tells yet a different story. Chart 3 tracks total government R&D and military R&D as percentages of GDP. Both rise steadily throughout the Eisenhower administration. These charts alone might explain Eisenhower's alarm over a "military-industrial complex" and a "scientific and technical elite"; as a percentage of GDP, military R&D quadrupled during his presidency. Thereafter, the numbers enter a gentle decline that continues with slight exception for the remainder of the Cold War. There is a blip for Vietnam, a steady increase in the Reagan years, and a final blip surrounding the Gulf War.

Chart 4 reinforces this story. It tracks military and total government R&D as percentages of federal expenditures. Unlike the case with total military spending, these numbers never return to their pre–Korean War levels. In essence, the United States spends proportionally less on the military than it did before the Cold War but proportionally more on R&D. The development of new military technology became a robust national strategy that not even the end of the Cold War could diminish.

The defense industry evolved to match government spending. In 1958, 30 of the companies in the top 50 spots on the *Fortune* 500 list of the largest industrial corporations also appeared on the list of the top 100 defense contractors.[28] Government contracts to universities, most of them military, vaulted those institutions to national prominence as well. Massachusetts Institute of Technology (MIT) and Johns Hopkins University, for example, held perennial positions on the list of leading defense contractors. Critics came to call it "the contract state."[29] Economist Seymour Melman warned that the United States, "if it is saved from

---

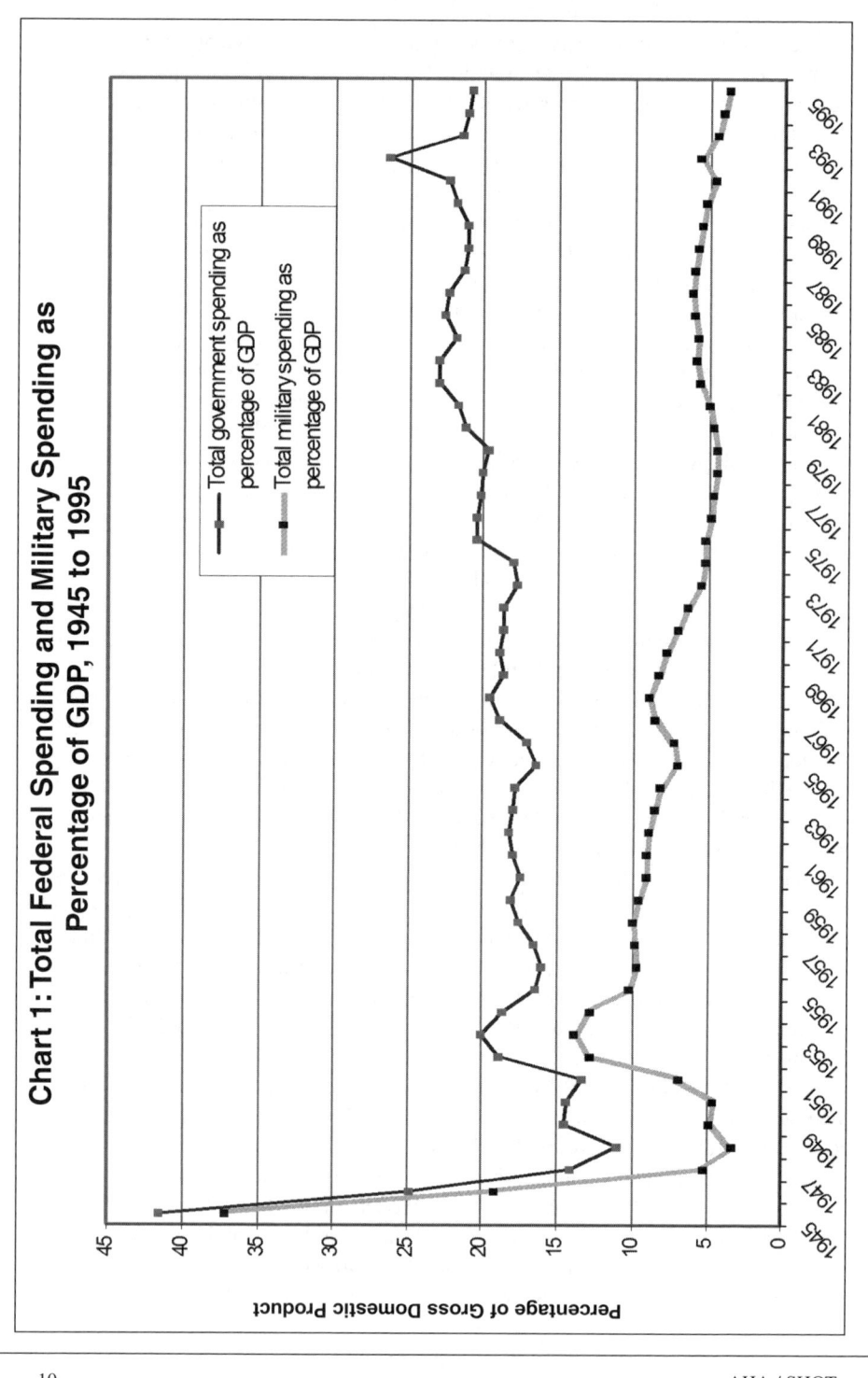

Chart 1: Total Federal Spending and Military Spending as Percentage of GDP, 1945 to 1995

Percentage of Gross Domestic Product

Total government spending as percentage of GDP

Total military spending as percentage of GDP

Chart 2: Military Spending as percentage of government spending, 1945 to 1995

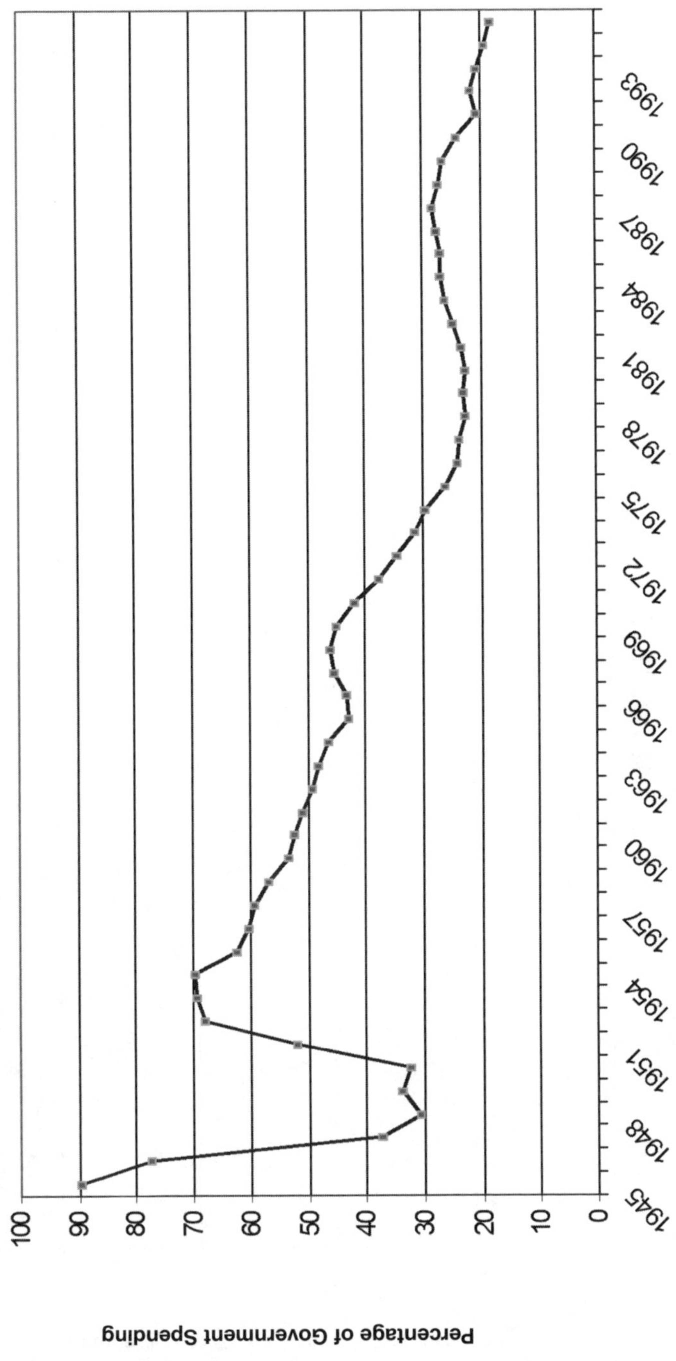

Percentage of Government Spending

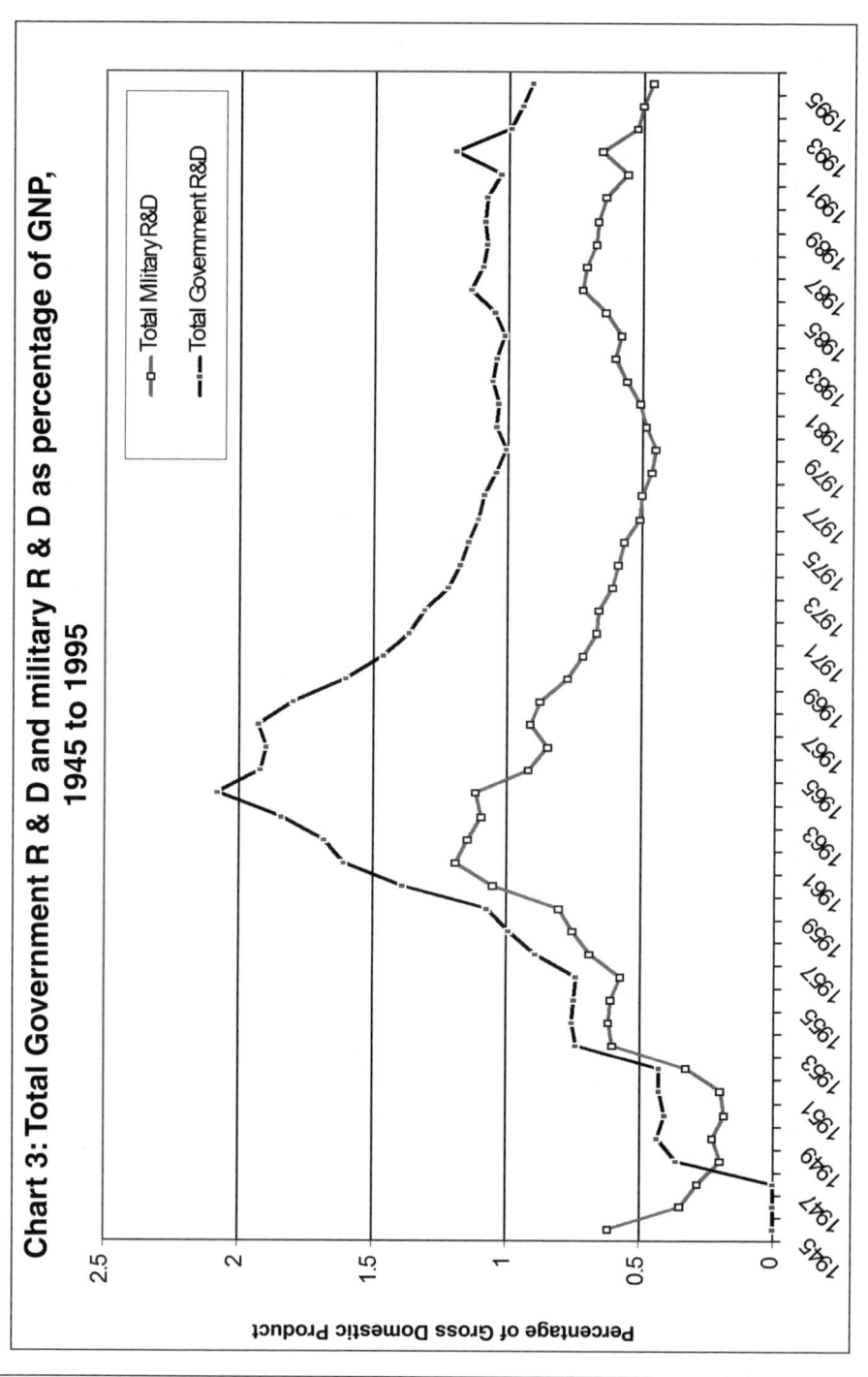

Chart 3: Total Government R & D and military R & D as percentage of GNP, 1945 to 1995

Legend: Total Military R&D; Total Government R&D

Y-axis: Percentage of Gross Domestic Product

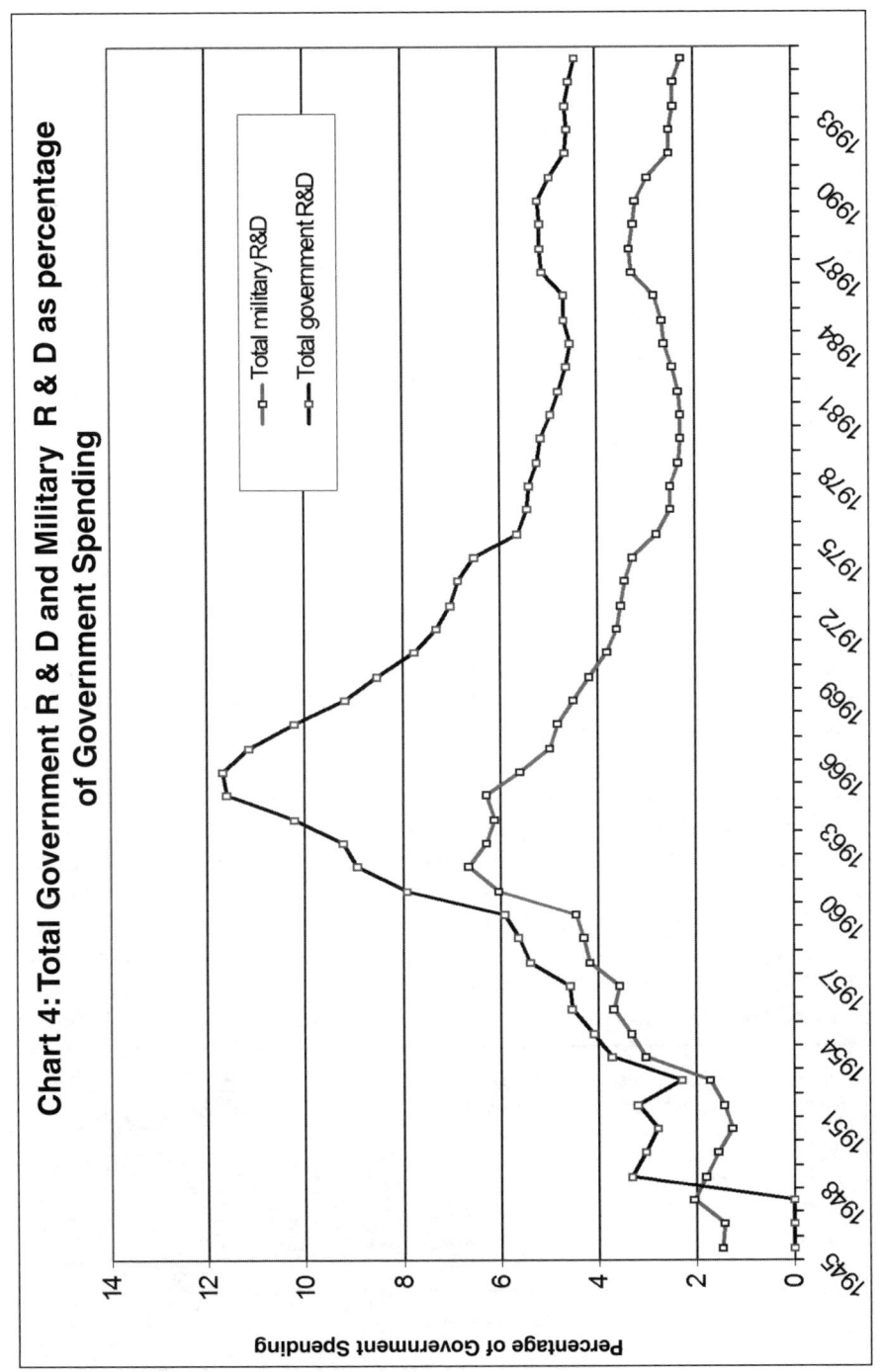

Chart 4: Total Government R & D and Military R & D as percentage of Government Spending

nuclear war, will surely become the guardian of a garrison-like society dominated by the Pentagon and its state-management."[30]

Eisenhower's "delta of power" became an arena in which powerful political and economic forces contended for defense contracts. Would-be contractors lobbied their legislative representatives to pressure the Defense Department in favor of their bids. Legislators sought defense contracts on their own initiative, both to bring dollars to their district and to encourage campaign contributions from constituent contractors. The military services curried favor with legislative allies by placing contracts in their states and districts. Finally, the services realized that distribution of contracts and subcontracts across a broad array of congressional districts provided political insulation against cancellation of their programs. The pork barrel of nineteenth-century American politics turned into a powerful, sophisticated, and complex infrastructure that presidents from Eisenhower to Clinton often found irresistible. Even after the Cold War was over, the administration of President Bill Clinton supported the construction of Seawolf submarines primarily as a jobs program for Groton, Connecticut, home of the manufacturer Electric Boat Company. This was not the first weapons system targeted at domestic politics and economics rather than a foreign adversary.

President Jimmy Carter, a former naval officer and a reform candidate for the presidency, discovered the power of the military-industrial complex in his fight over the B-1 bomber. Carter inherited from his predecessors a long-standing program to build a successor to the B-52, the workhorse of America's strategic bomber force and a mainstay of the air campaign in Vietnam. First proposed to President Eisenhower in 1957 as the B-70 Valkyrie, the airplane was repeatedly deferred or rejected either because its costs or capabilities were suspect or because the B-52 was still adequate. But Phoenix-like, the B-70 rose from the ashes, reinvented by the military-industrial complex as a cruise-missile-carrier, as a "Long Range Combat Aircraft," and as a "Strategic Weapons Launcher." President Carter thought he had terminated the program for good, but his successor, Ronald Reagan, especially sensitive to the aerospace industry in his home state of California, revived the airplane (now called the B-1) and put it into production in 1986. The last of the initial order of 100 planes came off the assembly line in

Figure 2. *The B-1 is pictured (in this artist's rendering) flying between its predecessor, the B-52 (top), and its successor, the B-2 stealth bomber (bottom). The B-1 finally went into production in 1986, almost thirty years after it was first proposed to President Eisenhower. Labeled the "born-again bomber" by journalist Nick Kotz, the B-1 demonstrated the sturdy resilience of the military-industrial complex in overcoming resistance to proposed weapons systems. (U.S. Air Force photo)*

1988, just in time for the end of the Cold War. At $280 million dollars apiece, more than ten times the projected price of the B-70 proposed to Eisenhower (three times the price in constant dollars), the aircraft never approached the performance capabilities promised for it.[31] Furthermore, it would have been obsolescent at birth had not its successor, the B-2 Stealth Bomber, been even later in development and far more over cost, rising finally to more than $2 billion per plane.

Stories such as this one illustrate two characteristics of Cold War technology. The first is obsolescence. U.S. weapons systems often competed with themselves. Instead of measuring U.S. technology against the capabilities of the Soviet Union or other potential adversaries, the Department of Defense often benchmarked their needs against an advancing wave of theoretical capability. The test of a weapons system was not its parity with the weapons systems of enemies or potential enemies but rather parity with the next generation of weapons systems that industry could envision. The United States had to develop the next generation because it could not run the risk that an adversary might steal a march. The system drove itself relentlessly to build weapons not because they were needed but because they were possible.

This criterion bred a kind of technological determinism, a second characteristic of Cold War weapons systems. The B-1, which journalist Nick Kotz called the "born-again bomber," seemed to have a life of its own. Once proposed, it proved impervious to politics, economics, failures of performance, or even the waning of the Cold War. But it was not the technology that persisted and prevailed; it was the complex. The web of war, politics, economics, and technology formed a cocoon that was proof against failure of any thread—lessening conflict, corrupt politics, bad economics, or failed technology. Weapons systems routinely came on line late, over cost, and under specifications. Promoters of military technology mastered the technique of "buying in," Washington jargon for empty promises sustained until the sunk costs in a project made it too embarrassing for Congress to cut it off. The B-1 was exceptional for its longevity and resilience, but it was hardly unique.

Nor did the phenomenon limit itself to the armed services. The civilian space program, another instrument of Cold War competition with the Soviet Union, adopted some of the same practices that characterized weapons development. The Apollo program succeeded in accomplishing the moon mission on time and on budget through a combination of capable management and adequate funding. NASA initially requested all the money it needed for Apollo, instead of asking for what the political market would bear. Then it solved its technical problems by pursuing multiple solutions, as the Manhattan Project had done during World War II. NASA funded alternative developments for risky components and designed redundancy into the complete system.

Even during Apollo, however, NASA's record for research and development slipped into the range experienced by the Department of Defense. Its space science projects from 1958 through March 1996 experienced average cost growth 220 percent above estimates.[32] The space shuttle proved to be a particularly glaring example. When NASA proposed this successor to the Saturn launch vehicle, neither Congress nor the administration of Richard Nixon supported the generous cushion of funding that Apollo had enjoyed. Forced to design to budget, NASA finally proposed a shuttle that could not possibly perform as promised.[33] It was a classic case of "buying in." When shuttle development ground to a halt in the Carter administration, NASA relied on the air force to win additional funding from the president. Like the B-1, the shuttle came in late, over cost, and under specifications. Many of the same players and imperatives that drove the military-industrial complex had produced another marvel of technology that the country had not wanted or requested.

Did the United States, therefore, become a militarized state during the Cold War?[34] Were elected civilian leaders still in control of government, or was the complex acting autonomously to produce technology of its own choosing? In 1941, political scientist Harold Lasswell had warned about "the garrison state, ... a world in which the specialists on violence are the most powerful group in society."[35] This possibility suggested itself to Lasswell when he learned of the Japanese bombing of China in 1937. He wondered if the subjection of civilians to military attack, what he called the "socialization of danger," would not empower the military to permanently organize society for war. The "specialist on violence," he suggested, might displace the businessman, the bureaucrat, and the politician atop "the power pyramid." C. Wright Mills's "power elite" might be militarized, paradoxically, by

> specialists on violence [who] are more preoccupied with the skills and attitudes judged characteristic of nonviolence. We anticipate the merging of skills, starting from the traditional accoutrements of professional soldier, moving toward the manager and promoter of large-scale civilian enterprise.[36]

Two trends converged in Lasswell's garrison state. On the one hand, a conventional militarization of society allowed uniformed officers and military considerations to gain purchase in the formulation of national policy. Those given to such fears could see the appointment of General George C. Marshall as secretary of state in the Truman administration as evidence of this trend, to say nothing of the election of General Eisenhower. On the other hand, civilian leaders elected and appointed to oversee the military were themselves imbued with many of the values Lasswell dreaded. Secretary of State John Foster Dulles envisioned a moral crusade against godless communism and was prepared to take the United States to the brink of Armageddon in defense of "security."

Lasswell's "merging of skills" reads like a prescription for selecting Charles E. Wilson as secretary of defense. His appointment by Dwight Eisenhower, the soldier-turned-university-president and then U.S. president, implied that what was good for the Defense Department was good for America. Indeed the military's infatuation with planned obsolescence came to resemble the automobile industry's embrace of tail fins and annual model changes. The militarization of the "power elite," the merging of skills foreseen by Lasswell, seemed complete when

Neil McElroy, president of Procter & Gamble Company, succeeded Wilson as secretary of defense. He raised the specter of weapons systems being sold like laundry soap. There was more than a little irony, then, in Eisenhower's warning against the military-industrial complex, and even a "garrison state," when his administration looked so much like the embodiment of these phenomena.[37]

Perhaps the most salient characteristic of the military-industrial complex in its heyday was the stunning contrast between its marvels of technological achievement and its wretched institutional excesses. The complex produced the arsenal that won the Cold War and contributed to the transformation of modern life. Reconnaissance satellites tracked the cars of Soviet officials on the streets of Moscow. The F-111 swing-wing attack bomber flew at two and a half times the speed of sound but landed slowly enough to put down on an aircraft carrier. Nuclear ballistic missile submarines eluded enemy detection for months on end while bristling with multi-warheaded missiles preprogrammed to deliver irresistible, cataclysmic retaliation against any attack on the vital interests of the United States. Ground-based ballistic missiles threatened targets thousands of miles away with accuracy measured in hundreds of meters. The Global Positioning Satellite system allowed American ground troops in the Gulf War of 1991 to navigate the pathless deserts of the Mesopotamian Valley with speed and accuracy that completely befuddled the indigenous soldiers. Smart weapons allowed American soldiers to stand out of harm's way and launch strikes at room-size targets while minimizing collateral damage. Stealth technology degraded the power of radar, one of the decisive weapons of World War II, allowing American aircraft to fly with impunity through the enemy's electronic defenses. Ballistic missile defense defied the best efforts of the military-industrial complex, but just the threat that the United States would attempt it contributed to the collapse of the Soviet Union. In the end, the complex built up an arsenal of conventional weapons and capabilities almost as destructive and decisive as the nuclear arms with which the country began the Cold War.

But that same complex also bred political, social, and economic scandal. Defense contractors charged $435 for a hammer and $1,868 for a toilet seat cover.[38] And the military paid. The "missile mess" of the Eisenhower administration suggested services more interested in competing with one another than with the Soviet Union. Security classification routinely masked information from the American public that was well known to the Soviet government. The nation stockpiled 32,000 nuclear warheads, enough to destroy the Soviet Union many times over. A revolving door shuffled defense and industry executives back and forth between conflicts of interest. Defense industries received corporate welfare and insulation from market forces. Many of Eisenhower's scientific-technical elite served the complex in the name of serving national security. "Defense intellectuals" and "beltway bandits" (companies in the vicinity of the highway encircling Washington, D.C., that specialize in contracting for government) provided support services for the complex.

The good news is that the military-industrial complex won the Cold War. For better or for worse, it produced the arsenal that sustained deterrence long enough for the democratic, free-market system to prevail over the authoritarian, command economy of the Soviet Union. The bad news is that the complex exacted a price. As Sovietologist George Kennan warned in 1946, the United States ran the risk in the Cold War of taking on the shape of the enemy, of becoming what it fought against. If the United States did not become a garrison state, as had seemed possible during the worst nights of the McCarthy era, it at least took on many of the aspects of a command economy. In the view of William McNeill, this is an economy driven not by market forces but by the imperatives of state policy. Technology was the focus of that imperative.

This particular combination of forces in Cold War America made Eisenhower's military-industrial complex unique. All industrialized states in the twentieth century have institutionalized some relationship between war and technology. Many states developed this relationship in the nineteenth century and even earlier. Only in the United States, however, did the concept of a military-industrial complex become part of the public debate and a historical event. Born in World War II, energized in the McCarthy era, labeled by Eisenhower, made salient in the anti-war movement of the Vietnam era, and defused by the waning of the Cold War, the military-industrial complex cut a swath through American history unmatched by the experience of any other nation. No country claimed as much for its military technology or achieved as much. No country worried more about the militarization of its institutions. No country was shaped as forcefully by the science and technology of war.

2

CIVIL-MILITARY RELATIONS

The military-industrial complex challenged civilian control of the military. The common plaint running through Lasswell's garrison state, Mills's power elite, and Eisenhower's farewell warning was abrogation of the country's constitutional and traditional commitment to civilian rule. Samuel P. Huntington's classic 1957 study, *The Soldier and the State*, had argued that military professionalism would keep servicemen loyal to civilian rule through the crisis of the Cold War, in spite of the politicization of the armed services wrought by mobilization of the state's resources.[39] But Eisenhower worried nonetheless, not that the military was being civilianized, but rather that some officers embraced, even sought out, the alliance with industry and Congress that undergird the military-industrial complex.

Participants in the complex pushed consistently for higher levels of defense spending. When Senator John Tower became secretary of defense in the new Reagan administration, he immediately held a press conference to call for annual defense budget increases of 9 percent over inflation; upon reflection he raised the number to 13 percent.[40] The question "how much is enough" pitted fiscal prudence against patriotism and loyalty. To suggest that a weapons system was not needed bordered on treason. Refusal of a military request for funding not only placed the nation's servicemen in harm's way, but it put the entire population at risk. Estimates of Soviet capabilities portrayed an adversary ten feet tall; calls for balance and moderation were dismissed as being "soft on communism."[41]

The struggle for civilian control of the military-industrial complex reached something of a nadir in the TFX project. Defense Secretary Robert McNamara brought to the Pentagon in 1961 his Ford Motor Company experience with rational management and econometric analysis, as well as his own entourage of "whiz kids." When they learned that both the air force and the navy sought funding for new-generation fighter-bombers, he insisted that they combine their development programs to build a single aircraft for both services. Deaf to pleas that air force planes should not be designed to land on aircraft carriers, McNamara insisted that cost-benefit analysis favored joint development. He was determined to accomplish what President Eisenhower's three secretaries of defense had failed to achieve: civilian control of the military.

Figure 3. *Determined to establish civilian control over the military-industrial complex, Defense Secretary Robert S. McNamara (1961–67) discounted the claims and prerogatives of service culture in favor of rational, cost-benefit analysis. (LBJ Library photo by Yoichi R. Okamoto)*

Variable-sweep wings provided a technical solution for the fundamental incompatibility between air force and navy specifications. If the aircraft's wings could be swept back for supersonic flight through enemy defenses and then swept forward for low-speed carrier landings, the same aircraft could serve both masters. Coincidentally, a NASA researcher advanced a novel design concept to solve the knotty mechanical and aerodynamical problems of variable sweep, and General Dynamics set about building the TFX. Over the protests and lamentations of air force and naval officers, and the critical scrutiny of some congressmen and aerospace industrialists, the project produced the F-111. Characteristically and predictably, the plane came in late, over cost, and under specifications, but it worked. The navy version was canceled before going operational, but air force versions flew limited missions in Vietnam, the 1986 raid on Libya, and the Gulf War before the plane was retired in 1996. McNamara's critics insist that his attempt to dictate joint development displayed a profound ignorance of navy and air force missions, but scholars have found that the navy applied its technical criteria capriciously.[41] "The technical disagreement," says political scientist Robert Art, "really represented a struggle by the air force and the navy to keep their identities separate, distinct, and autonomous."[43]

The evolution of ballistic missile guidance demonstrates the ways in which the military-industrial imperative could actually transform American strategic policy, a realm of civilian preeminence. In the 1960s, the United States adopted a policy of counter-value targeting for its strategic nuclear weapons. If the Soviet Union attacked the United States or its vital interests abroad, the United States would retaliate by attacking Soviet infrastructure—its cities, industrial base, and economic resources. At the time, American intercontinental ballistic missiles simply did not have sufficient accuracy to target the Soviet Union's strategic forces, i.e., its missiles and bombers, which, in any case, might already be in flight to the United States by the time retaliation was ordered. The threat of this counter-value retaliation created the aptly named policy MAD—mutual assured destruction—which saw the superpowers through some of their most dangerous confrontations.

Impervious to this policy, the military-industrial complex worked through the 1960s and 1970s to improve missile accuracy. This campaign was driven not by

Figure 4. *The F-111 swing-wing fighter bomber was a technical success but a programmatic failure. The navy version was canceled before going operational; the air force version saw only limited service. The aircraft is more important historically as the battleground on which Defense Secretary Robert McNamara fought the navy and the air force over civilian control of the military. (U.S. Air Force photo)*

the Soviet threat to American national security, but by interservice rivalry between the air force and the navy. Both services sought a share of the strategic nuclear mission. The navy initially found itself at a disadvantage, because missiles launched from its mobile submarines were inherently less accurate than missiles launched from fixed silos on land. The navy, therefore, supported research on improved guidance. The air force followed suit, not because it served national interests but because it served the parochial interests of the air force and its contractors. In the end, both programs achieved marvels of technological sophistication, guidance systems that could direct ballistic missiles thousands of miles and land them within hundreds of meters of the aiming point. In fact, the guidance became so good that the United States unwittingly developed the capability to attack the Soviet Union's land-based strategic forces in a preemptive first strike. This had not been the national intent, nor was it in the national interest. But the military-industrial complex had produced the result on its own initiative. The capability alarmed the Soviet Union and set off the Soviet arms buildup of the 1970s that so exercised the Reagan administration and spawned another round in the arms race. Civilian policymakers watched helplessly as their chosen strategic policy was obviated by military research and development.[44]

The TFX and ballistic missile guidance programs are only the most notorious of the instances in which the military-industrial complex challenged traditional civilian control of the military. Routine behavior such as the placing of defense contracts, the hyping of new projects to get Congress to buy in, and the coordinated exaggeration of the Soviet threat by both military and industry all lessened the autonomy of civilian policymakers and increased the influence of the military in decisions ranging from the federal budget and taxes to foreign policy and aid to education.

The military also undermined civilian autonomy by creating a parallel infrastructure to challenge the counsel of civilian institutions. The services created their own think tanks, such as Rand Corporation. They sustained pre-war research establishments such as the Naval Research Laboratory, which operated in the traditional civilian realm of basic research. They remained the primary sponsors of laboratories at research universities, such as the Applied Physics Laboratory at the Johns Hopkins University. In some cases they funded semi-independent spin-off institutions, such as MIT's Lincoln Laboratory. They set up their own advisory committees of civilian scientists and engineers, such as the Air Force Science Advisory Committee. The technical experts who found themselves in the military orbit provided excellent, usually independent, advice. But as the sponsor, the Department of Defense could always cancel contracts, terminate memberships, and restrict funding. By controlling support for these institutions and individuals, the military cultivated its own experts to challenge the normal order of civil-military relations.

The military also constrained civilian control by limiting the flow of information. Technical secrets were among the most closely guarded of the Cold War. Policy, plans, and intelligence were the normal stuff of classification, but technical information allowed your enemy to duplicate and defeat your weapons.

Entirely new categories of security clearance—Special Access Programs and Sensitive Compartmented Information—displaced "top secret" in the hierarchy of classification. When Robert Oppenheimer's security clearance was lifted in the McCarthy era because his opposition to fusion weapons suggested softness on communism, his career as a nuclear physicist ended. As the armed forces came to see more and more technologies as crucial to national security, the web of secrecy spread out from weapons systems into the civilian economy. The Export Administration Act of 1979 required the government "to restrict the export of goods and technology which [*sic*] would make a significant contribution to the military potential of any other country."[45] The following year, the Department of Defense prepared its first "critical technologies list," which was, of course, classified. The unclassified version published in 1984 identified twenty critical "arrays of know-how," ranging from computer hardware, software, and networking to instrumentation, telecommunications, and "vehicular technology."[46] By 1991, the list had changed significantly and the focus had shifted to promoting these technologies while at the same time ensuring "protection of scientific and technological achievements from transfer to unauthorized parties."[47] The program called for the government to monitor the dissemination of "critical" information whether or not that knowledge had been produced with government funding.

These unprecedented restraints on technology transfer coincided with an enlargement of the scope of security classification. Executive Order 12356 of 1982 led to more than 19 million "classification decisions" in fiscal year 1984 and a backlash from the scientific and technical communities,[48] which complained of government infringement on free speech and intrusion into the academy, the laboratory, and the conference hall.[49] In Senator Daniel Patrick Moynihan's assessment, the United States had moved from "a culture of secrecy" in the McCarthy era to "the routinization of secrecy" through the remainder of the Cold War, and beyond.[50] Librarian Herbert N. Foerstel estimated that the United States published about half the world's unclassified technical information in the 1970s, less than 25 percent by 1993.[51]

The identification of critical technologies and the assignment of security classification to nondefense research contributed to the blurring of distinctions between civilian and military. Beginning in 1991, a National Critical Technologies list subsumed the military version, reflecting "a highly interdependent economy with substantial overlap between civilian and defense applications."[52] Uniformed officers evolved from warriors to "managers of violence." The development of the Polaris missile submarine produced a management system known as Program Evaluation Review Technique.[53] More effective at impressing congressmen than aiding management, the process nonetheless lent the impression of rational development and spread to other nondefense agencies. Drawing on experience developing bombers in World War II, the air force created a comparable system, "concurrency," to accelerate development of the Atlas missile. When NASA's Apollo program fell behind schedule in 1967 after the fatal fire in the 204 module, the agency imported retired air force general Samuel Phillips to restore order.

Phillips applied concurrency to Apollo under the rubric of "all-up testing."[54] It saved the Apollo program but eroded the perception of NASA as a civilian agency.

The blurring of distinctions between military and civilian technologies finally gave way to open pursuit of "dual-use technologies." These had both military and civilian applications. They are as old as roads, ships, wagons, and hunting instruments. Not until the Cold War, however, did the United States embrace them as a national goal. Computers offer the best example of a general-purpose technology developed with huge infusions of military funding. ENIAC (Electronic Numerical Integrator and Communicator), the first general-purpose electronic computer in the United States, was built to compute ballistic tables; it was then turned to calculations for nuclear weapons development. The IBM AN/SFQ-7 pioneered networking for the SAGE continental air defense system and then went on to be the prototype for the SABRE commercial airline reservation system. Magnetic core memory appeared first on the Whirlwind computer, developed at MIT for the navy and the air force. The Defense Advanced Research Projects Agency for many years provided the chief source of support for artificial intelligence research in the United States. It also led the development of computer networks, computer graphics, and massive parallel processing architecture.

At first, the military supported such research in order to develop technologies for direct military application. By the 1990s, however, the services found themselves migrating toward support of some commercial technologies. Breaking with the long pattern of military support for highly specialized technology custom-designed for military applications, the defense establishment came to see that it could leverage its own budget by helping the market to develop products appropriate for both military and civilian applications. Defense

Figure 5. *Two women "program" ENIAC by physically wiring its component devices in the order required for the problem they are working. Developed during World War II to compute ballistic trajectories, ENIAC was the first electronic, general-purpose, automatic computer. It helped to establish a pattern of military support for computer research that continued through the Cold War. (U.S. Army photo)*

procurement could then realize economies of scale, such as the rapid price drops experienced in consumer electronics. This philosophy allowed the American military to send its soldiers into the Gulf War of 1991 with off-the-shelf laptop computers. The military continued to develop technologies the market would not support, such as high-performance computers and exotic materials, but its gradual drift toward dual-use technologies nonetheless further blurred the distinction between civilian and military.

3

STATE AND INDUSTRY

Until World War II, the United States developed many of its military technologies in its own arsenals and laboratories. Interchangeable parts, for example, were perfected in the Springfield, Massachusetts, armory. Eli Whitney had introduced them to the U.S. government and received a contract to deliver 10,000 muskets during the war of 1812. Perfecting interchangeability, however, proved more difficult and more expensive than Whitney had envisioned. The idea was brought to fruition only through painstaking and costly development in an arsenal insulated from market forces. Even there, it met resistance from entrenched guild forces reluctant to change age-old patterns of hand craftsmanship.[55] From the arsenal, the concept of interchangeability spread to the private sector through sewing machines, bicycles, and finally the automobile assembly line of Henry Ford.[56]

Of course the military traditionally purchased from contractors as well—steel producers, shipyards, and munitions manufacturers. But it often looked to its own arsenals and laboratories for innovation and the establishment of standards. From naval ordnance at the Washington Naval Yard to aeronautical research at McCook Field (later Wright-Patterson Air Force Base) in Dayton, Ohio, to ship design at the David Taylor Model Basin outside Washington, D.C., the military services supported their own research establishments and seldom turned to industry or universities for innovation.

All that changed in World War II. Rejecting the failed World War I model of commissioning scientists and engineers and bringing them onto active duty for the war emergency, the government created the National Defense Research Committee in 1939, and transformed it into the Office of Scientific Research and Development (OSRD) in 1941. Under the leadership of Vannevar Bush, former dean of engineering at the Massachusetts Institute of Technology and most recently the president of the Carnegie Institution in Washington, OSRD recruited scientists and engineers for the war effort but left them in place in their home institutions. Through contracts with industries and universities, the government commissioned the best technical talent in the country and built up research infrastructure around them. The Radiation Laboratory at MIT, for example, became the nucleus of radar research in the United States, one of a network of sites working on more than 100 radar projects ranging from airborne anti-submarine radar to the proximity fuse, which allowed bombs and shells to explode when they came near their targets.

At the close of World War II, Vannevar Bush recommended to President Franklin Roosevelt a National Research Establishment to continue the wartime pattern of supporting the nation's scientists and engineers by contracting for research essential to national security and economic development. That recommendation ultimately led to the creation of the National Science Foundation in 1950, the agency responsible for basic or pure scientific research. The concept of contracting for military research survived, both in facilities such as Johns Hopkins University's Applied Physics Laboratory and MIT's Lincoln Laboratory, and in ad hoc contracts with industries and universities enlisted for specific undertakings.

The arsenal system also survived, especially for those research projects requiring especially expensive facilities and equipment. For example, the nuclear research and production facilities of World War II's Manhattan Project survived the war in only slightly altered form. Los Alamos Laboratory, where the Hiroshima and Nagasaki bombs were designed and built, continued to conduct weapons research in the Cold War under the management of the University of California. Sandia National Laboratories grew up next door, a commercial contractor responsible now for building the nation's nuclear weapons. A new Lawrence Livermore National Laboratory joined the University of California at Berkeley's wartime Radiation Laboratory in 1952 to expand the range of weapons research being conducted under contract through the university. The air force built an entire suite of wind tunnels at Arnold Engineering Development Center in Tulahoma, Tennessee, to conduct for itself the testing and innovation previously done by the National Advisory Committee for Aeronautics.

In spite of the state-of-the-art equipment and lavish budgets at these and other military laboratories, government research facilities lost some of the luster they had enjoyed prior to World War II. They were unable to overcome the long-standing perception that the best scientists and engineers gravitated to prestigious university and industry appointments, while second-class researchers accepted bureaucratic positions with the government. Arsenals, it was widely believed, were staffed by place-fillers and mediocrities who embraced the security of civil-service tenure in lieu of competing in the great marketplace of ideas and achievement. In spite of anecdotal evidence to the contrary, innovation seemed to spring from universities and industry, while routine, pedestrian results emerged from government laboratories.

This perception fueled creation of a two-tier reward system, in which the most distinguished scientists and engineers held high-paying positions in academia and industry, supplementing their salaries with lucrative government contracts and consultancies, while lesser researchers worked at civil-service scale in government laboratories. The power and pitfalls of this system were nowhere more in evidence than in the rise of Ramo-Wooldridge Corporation, a classic case study of the military-industrial complex at its best and worst. Simon Ramo and Dean Wooldridge were scientists-turned-engineers in the Electronics Division of Hughes Aircraft. In 1953, Trevor Gardner, special assistant to the secretary of the air force for research and development, became enamored with their "excellent leadership" of Hughes's Falcon air-to-air missile program, which he considered to be "a model for the rest of the military technology industry."[57] When Gardner sought staff support for a blue-ribbon Strategic Missiles Evaluation Committee, known by its code name of Teapot Committee, he turned to the two engineers. They left their Hughes jobs to set up Ramo-Wooldridge Corporation and accept a letter contract from Gardner. The new corporation provided technical services to

Figure 6. *Simon Ramo teamed with colleague Dean Wooldridge to parlay a consultancy with the famed Teapot Committee into a contract with their start-up company to provide management services for the Atlas missile program. Atlas was a great success, but their cozy relationship with the air force and the high profits they realized prompted a congressional investigation. (Special Collections, J. Willard Marriott Library, University of Utah)*

the Teapot Committee and drafted its report. The Teapot Committee recommended that the Atlas intercontinental ballistic missile program be accelerated on a crash basis. But the air force, newly created in 1947, had not the staff, facilities, or expertise to run a program on the scale envisioned by the Teapot Committee. In short, the arsenal was not up to the job. So the air force hired Ramo-Wooldridge to assume "technical responsibility" for Atlas.

Needing capital and personnel, Ramo-Wooldridge merged with Thompson Products Company of Cleveland, which put up half a million dollars, while Ramo and Wooldridge retained 51 percent control of their firm for an investment of $6,750 each. The company's fee for its initial contract with the air force was 14.3 percent of the contract cost, more than twice the average fee for R&D contracts in the Department of Defense. When the company reorganized again in 1958, to become Thompson-Ramo-Wooldridge, Inc. (TRW), the young engineers' initial investments of $6,750 had grown to $3,150,000 each. The Atlas program succeeded, but at the price of high salaries and alarming profits for TRW.

The facts of the Ramo-Wooldridge story are not in doubt; most of them came out during the course of a 1959 congressional investigation into the company's relationship with the air force. But what do they mean? Ramo-Wooldridge Corporation may be seen as a product of privilege and favoritism, exacting unwarranted profits from an indecent conflict of interest. But the Atlas missile may be seen as a technological marvel resulting from a unique alliance of free-enterprise capitalism and government sponsorship. Eschewing the socialist model of many other industrialized states, such as Japan and France, to say nothing of the command economy of the Soviet Union, the United States linked the public and private sector in a cooperative scheme that retained strong aspects of both. The government could make enormous capital investments in long-term projects benefiting the commonwealth, and industry could mobilize the private sector for discrete undertakings. Among the many controversial aspects of this relationship between industry and the state, four may be singled out as particularly troubling and ambiguous.

The "revolving door" between public and private service allowed cross-fertilization of the two sectors and invited conflict of interest. Military officers retired and went to work for the companies whose contracts they had recently managed. Corporate executives took leave from their companies to enter government service in positions dealing with their former and future employers. Changing places had much to recommend it. When Simon Nora and Alain Minc surveyed the computer industry for the French government in 1980, they concluded that the great advantage held by the United States in the world market resulted from the "thick fabric" of interwoven American institutions. Computer professionals from academia, industry, and government collaborated with one another and moved seamlessly among the different realms of computer activity. Nora and Minc believed that institutional rigidity in France precluded such healthy cross-fertilization there. But the other side of this coin revealed collusion, corruption, and conflict of interest. An "old boy" network—in its heyday the military-industrial complex was predominantly male—swapped jobs, information, and confidences in the sure belief that what was good for the defense industry was good for America, and vice versa. Competition was intense, between companies, between services, and between educational institutions. But barriers between these realms were porous.

A second controversial aspect of the military-industrial relationship was corporate welfare. Believing that national security depended upon a wide and diverse infrastructural base, government officials distributed defense contracts so as to sustain multiple suppliers of critical products and services. Lockheed Aircraft Corporation received the contract for the C-5A transport over rival Boeing Corporation because Boeing had plenty of business at the time and Lockheed was struggling. Air force leadership overruled its own technical panel to make this award.[58] Such tinkering with the free market made good sense militarily, but it flirted with the national socialism that so many defenders of the military-industrial complex professed to abhor. In short, it turned many defense contractors into quasi-nationalized industries sustained for reasons of state policy, as opposed to market competitiveness. Seldom is this model credited with promoting innovation.

The military-industrial relationship also distorted market forces. Corporations, such as the Martin Company, limited themselves almost exclusively to military contracts. This condition heightened the impact of government specifications and lowered the impulse to innovate. Such companies were more likely to give the military services whatever they demanded, whether or not it was technologically sound, and less likely to develop new products for the marketplace. On the other hand, military impact on the aerospace industry has also produced commercial spin-offs of great value. The Boeing 747, for example, commercialized the company's failed attempt to win a government contract for military cargo planes, just as the air force's C-135 was a converted Boeing 707. R&D contracts were one of the ways in which the government contributed to the rise of the American aerospace industry, the world leader throughout the Cold War.

The government shaped defense-related markets in other ways as well. Government standards, specifications, accounting practices, protocols, and record-keeping influenced the corporate style and worldview of defense contractors. On the one hand, the government might require levels of performance that the market would not support, as it did, for example, in anti-lock braking systems first developed for military aircraft and then transferred to the commercial automobile market. On the other hand, it might also promote refinements of technology more expensive than they are worth, as was the case with the V-22 Osprey. Defense Secretary Dick Cheney told Congress in 1989 that the military simply could not afford these innovative tilt-wing aircraft, then projected to cost $25 billion over the coming decade. Congress made the armed forces buy the aircraft anyhow.

Finally, the intimate working relationship between the military services and the defense industry invited outright corruption. Perhaps the most notorious case was the C-5A scandal, noted both for the flagrance of the misconduct and for the denial of the problem. In 1965, Lockheed Aircraft received the $3 billion contract to produce an aircraft capable of takeoff and landing at unpaved airstrips, cruising at 600 miles per hour, and lifting more than 200,000 pounds of cargo. By 1971, the cost of each airplane had swollen to almost three times the original bid. What really set the case apart, however, was the craven politics of the senators and congressmen whose states and districts profited from the contract. Representative Mendell Rivers (D-SC) went so far as to threaten a colleague on the House floor with loss of military jobs in his home district. The air force compounded the public embarrassment by insisting that nothing was amiss. The civil servant who brought the scandal to light was punished for his disclosures.

More than delays and cost overruns plagued the C-5A. It was also a technological disappointment. Upon delivery, the giant aircraft was found to have wing defects that limited cargo capacity to 100,000 pounds, less than half the prescribed load. Defective engine mounts precluded full opening of the throttles, eliminating flight at full speed and takeoff and landing from unimproved runways. Poor landing gear kept the plane from putting down in a crosswind. Other failures further limited operational capability. Research and development on cutting-edge technology often produces delays and cost overruns. But if the process does not generate the expected technological advances, then the whole relationship between industry and the state falls under a cloud of suspicion.

Figure 7. *The C-5A military transport differed in degree but not kind from other Pentagon R&D programs. Costing almost three times it original estimate, the plane could carry only half the weight predicted and it could not land, as promised, on unimproved airstrips. The civil servant who revealed these and other shortcomings of the program was punished for his disclosures. (U.S. Air Force photo)*

4

AMONG GOVERNMENT AGENCIES

Within the federal government, the military-industrial complex spread its influence far beyond the confines of the Department of Defense. Most of the government agencies to feel its impact operated in technical realms, but even diplomacy and the environment were vulnerable. Foreign aid to developing nations often took the form of credits for purchases of U.S. military arms and equipment. Allies such as Israel demanded state-of-the-art American weapons to fight their Arab neighbors, who were armed largely with Soviet weapons. American arms manufacturers sought licenses to sell their wares abroad, seeking economies of scale through longer production runs. And all sales of American military technology gave the Department of State leverage with the purchasing countries, which would need spare parts, technical assistance, and training to maintain and operate the equipment. In short, the military-industrial complex produced a cornucopia of sought-after technology that the Department of State manipulated in pursuit of policy goals. Sometimes, however, the economic-industrial imperative came into conflict with avowed national policy and the State Department found itself mediating conflicts in which both sides were armed with American weapons.[59]

The Environmental Protection Agency received from the military-industrial complex powerful tools of monitoring, regulation, and enforcement. Earth-resources satellites, for example, drew upon military rocket, satellite, microelectronic, and sensor technology to detect water and soil pollution and to monitor runoff from winter snows. But the EPA confronted national security priorities in trying to root out pollution at government nuclear facilities. During the Cold War, nuclear weapons plants across the country are estimated to have contaminated 475 billion gallons of ground water. The Department of Energy estimates that it will spend $147 billion over 75 years to clean up 113 sites. The military services were similarly exempt from countless other environmental regulations, ranging from exhaust emissions to noise control. The only defense the military can claim is that the whole government has been guilty, from the U.S. Mint to the National Parks. As one environmental monitor put it, "the government remains the nation's premier environmental felon."[60]

Nowhere was the impact of the military-industrial complex felt more profoundly than in the quasi-military world of intelligence.[61] The arms and equipment needed by the United States were determined in part by the capabilities and intentions of the Soviet Union. The perverse logic of the Cold War convinced hardliners in both the United States and the Soviet Union that those determinants could be reduced to one: capabilities. The worst case was simply assumed for enemy intentions. Intentions were subjective; capabilities were matters of fact, or so the argument went. Attention therefore focused on the "force structure" of the Soviet Union, with an eye to assuring that U.S. force structure provided an adequate deterrent. If the Soviet Union developed a Mach 2 fighter plane, such as the MIG-21, then the United States had to have a Mach 2+ fighter, the F-4, or better yet, the Mach 2.5 F-15. If the Soviet Union developed an intercontinental ballistic missile with guidance accuracy of 100 meters, then the United States had to harden its missile silos to withstand 2,000 pounds per square inch of overpressure. If Soviet sonar improved its sensitivity, then U.S. nuclear submarines had to have propellers virtually free of noise-producing cavitation. The arms race of the Cold War was driven in large measure by the intelligence each side had about the other's capabilities. Seldom was it constrained by subjective judgments about how the enemy intended to use its arsenal.

This competition put a premium on the intelligence itself. Service roles and missions would rise and fall on the perception of an enemy threat. If ground-based missiles and bombers were vulnerable to preemptive first strikes, this raised the stock of the navy's ballistic missile submarines. If Soviet armored forces posed a threat to Europe, then anti-tank weapons and close air support gained purchase in the United States. If the Soviets developed a workable anti-satellite missile, then a new and independent U.S. space command might be required to maintain the growing military infrastructure in earth orbit.

For all these reasons, intelligence became politicized. The Central Intelligence Agency (CIA), formed in 1947 to provide the president with neutral and competent intelligence, found itself besieged. Individual services dissented from its "national intelligence estimates" and offered their own interpretations to the president and the National Security Council. The Department of Defense created its own Defense Intelligence Agency (DIA) to gather and interpret information in parallel with the CIA. Aircraft and then satellite reconnaissance became so important that a separate, independent agency, the National Reconnaissance Office (NRO), was spun off to conduct that business. It too became a stepchild of the military-industrial complex, relying on most of the same contractors and consultants, and weaving another warp of thick fabric. Still another technological spinoff appeared in 1952 when the National Security Agency (NSA) set up shop apart from the CIA to conduct electronic surveillance of the world's communications. When the CIA first publicly disclosed the annual intelligence budget of the United States in 1997, it was revealed to be $26.6 billion, much of it invested in the development, maintenance, and exploitation of high technology.[62] Everything from supercomputers to sensing devices to artificial intelligence for machine translation and photo interpretation fed on the intelligence imperative.

Few civilian federal agencies have experienced such a close and ambiguous relationship with the military-industrial complex as NASA. Intended by President Eisenhower to keep the military from capturing the national space mission and militarizing the heavens, NASA tried from the outset to distance itself from the Department of Defense. It stressed the priority of space science. It left reconnaissance to the military services. It invited international cooperation and openness. And it filtered its military relations through an innocuous and efficient Aeronautics and Astronautics Coordinating Board.

But it was always a tough sell. In the late 1950s and early 1960s, NASA flew its missions on military missiles converted to launch vehicles, its astronauts were military test pilots, and its satellites were indistinguishable from the reconnaissance spacecraft that were one of the most poorly kept secrets of the Cold War. Indeed, the first U.S. satellite reconnaissance program, *Corona*, flew under the cover of being a NASA science project, *Discoverer*. When U-2 pilot Gary Powers was shot down on a spy mission over the Soviet Union on the eve of the 1960 summit conference, NASA Public Affairs Officer Walter Bonney insisted that Powers had strayed off course on a NASA weather mission. That cover story evaporated when Powers was captured and confessed; with it went much of NASA's credibility as an independent agency innocent of Cold War machinations.

Even as NASA grew in independence and stature during the Apollo program of the 1960s, its ties to the military remained visible. It absorbed the army's Redstone Arsenal and renamed it in honor of General George C. Marshall. It continued to fly its test aircraft out of a facility spun off from Edwards Air Force Base in California, and it created its own space launch facility at Cape Canaveral, next to Patrick Air Force Base. When the Apollo program got into trouble, it imported an air force general to turn things around with an air force management scheme. At the end of the Apollo program, when it was trying to sell the shuttle as a "follow-on" vehicle, it designed the orbiter to fly air force reconnaissance missions in order to get much-needed military support for the project. When the shuttle faced cancellation in the Carter administration, the air force was once more enlisted to save it. Though NASA moved toward civilian astronauts and its own family of launch vehicles, it never lost its close ties to the military. Nor was

Space Shuttle Challenger

Challenger is photographed in orbit from a camera aboard a just released satellite

Figure 8. *NASA's space shuttle Challenger is photographed in orbit from a camera aboard a satellite it has just released. The shuttle was designed to accommodate the air force's reconnaissance satellite program. The payload bay was made big enough to hold the largest projected satellite and the wing plan was designed to allow the shuttle to return to earth from any orbit. The air force repaid NASA by supporting the shuttle program until the Challenger was destroyed on launch in 1986, leaving the country without an adequate launch vehicle. (NASA photo)*

it immune to developing a relationship with the aerospace industry that became hard to distinguish from the military's. Indeed, NASA even imitated some of the military's contracting techniques, not only technical schemes such as cost-plus-fixed-fee contracting but also political techniques such as "buying in" and distributing subcontracts by congressional districts. Just as the space program was a continuation of the Cold War by other means, so too was NASA's relationship with the aerospace industry a continuation of the military-industrial complex by other means.[63]

Nuclear power provides another instance of a critical national technology with dual-use potential that found itself firmly rooted in the military-industrial complex. Believing that the atom was too important to be left to the generals, the United States created the Atomic Energy Commission (AEC) in 1946, to succeed the wartime Manhattan Project and to oversee both the military and the civilian development of this promising and frightening technology. In the early years, the civilian commissioners nonetheless focused on military development of nuclear power, contributing to passage of a new Atomic Energy Act in 1954 stressing civilian use of the atom. This reform notwithstanding, the military imperative retained a strong hold on the agency and guided its future. The AEC promoted and launched commercial nuclear power in the United States during the 1960s and oversaw a great surge in plant construction known as the great bandwagon movement. Companies such as General Electric, which had pioneered military development of the atom in nuclear propulsion for naval vessels, converted that technology into turn-key, light-water-reactor plants that promised, in the words of Atomic Energy Commissioner Lewis L. Strauss, "power too cheap to meter."

The public, however, had difficulty dissociating the commercial reactor down the road from the mushroom cloud over Bikini Atoll. "Nuclear fear," historian Spencer Weart's term, permeated popular culture and tainted the perception of commercial nuclear power. Anti-nuclear activism of the late 1960s and early 1970s, augmented by the nascent environmental movement and concern for nuclear waste, derailed the great bandwagon movement and arrested the commercial nuclear power industry in the United States. While other countries such as France and Japan proceeded apace with the commercial development of nuclear power, the United States turned away from this technology for the remainder of the twentieth century. In no small measure, the reversal of course resulted from associations in the public mind between commercial nuclear power on the one hand and the bomb and the military-industrial complex on the other.

In an effort to regain civilian control of this technology, the U.S. government experimented with other institutional arrangements in the 1970s and 1980s. The AEC was broken up in an attempt to separate its conflicting responsibilities for regulation and promotion of nuclear energy. The Nuclear Regulatory Commission thereafter oversaw civilian nuclear power, but exercised little authority over military facilities and programs. The Energy Research and Development Administration took up promotion of national energy resources, including nuclear, but found itself absorbed by the Department of Energy (DoE) in 1977. Responsibility for producing the nation's nuclear arsenal migrated to the DoE, as did many veterans of the old AEC weapons programs. The power of civilian commissioners to control the weapons program remained a source of controversy throughout the Cold War and beyond. When the environmental abuses of the weapons laboratories were made public in the 1990s, it became clear that national security had trumped civilian oversight in the AEC and its successor agencies. The impact of the military-industrial complex on the executive branch of government reached far beyond the Department of Defense.

5

THE SCIENTIFIC-TECHNICAL COMMUNITY

President Eisenhower's warning about a "scientific technological elite" surprised and shocked the scientific community. Eisenhower had created a President's Science Advisory Committee in the wake of Sputnik, and he developed a great respect and affection for the scientists and engineers who served him in that capacity. What troubled him was the prospect not only of the growing power of such experts over public policy but also the related "prospect of domination of the nation's scholars by Federal employment, project allocations, and the power of money."[64]

Nowhere was that danger more evident than in the nation's universities. Stanford University and MIT rose to national prominence on a wave of government funding. Less visibly but nonetheless substantially, the University of Washington became the second largest university defense contractor (behind MIT) by expanding on the model of its World War II Applied Physics Laboratory. Lincoln Laboratory, created by MIT in 1951 to develop an air defense system for the air force, quickly expanded into other areas of defense contracting. In 1958 it spun off MITRE Corporation to do its systems engineering. By 1986, Lincoln had spun off 48 companies, totaling $8.6 billion in annual sales and employing more than 100,000 people. Professor Charles Stark Draper's Instrumentation Laboratory, in MIT's Department of Aeronautical Engineering, rivaled Lincoln Laboratory by the early 1960s and dwarfed its parent department. By 1965 it had spun off 27 companies with sales totaling $14 million and employees reaching 900.[65] In 1989, three universities were among the top 50 research-and-development contractors for the Department of Defense: MIT (13), Johns Hopkins (17), and the University of California at San Diego (43). Also on the list were MITRE Corporation (18) and Draper Laboratories (28).[66] Bolt, Beranek, and Newman, a Cambridge consulting firm specializing in acoustics and computers, became something of a halfway house for MIT faculty and students venturing into the technical marketplace. In the 1950s and 1960s Stanford was playing an equally decisive role in launching the Stanford Industrial Park and Silicon Valley.[67] At these centers of excellence, as they were called by the computer research community at the Department of Defense's Advanced Research Projects Agency, and at other universities around the country, academia blended with the military-industrial complex in ways that blurred the boundaries between them.

In one sense, this development was natural and positive. Academia, after all, made up one of the major threads of that "thick fabric" that Nora and Minc credited with American computer achievement. The issue that alarmed Eisenhower was proportion. Would the government, and especially the military, come to play too large a role in university policy, and would scientists and engineers establish unofficial rule over a Washington technocracy increasingly driven by technological imperatives? Many scholars examining the influence of military funding on scientific and technological development perceive a subtle but profound skewing of research agendas. Paul Forman, for example, has argued that scientists were tempted, if not forced, to put aside the most interesting and challenging questions in favor of the questions that came with research support attached.[68] Paul Edwards has argued that military support of computer research imbued this technology with a command-and-control ethos from which civilian applications have been unable to escape.[69] The independence of university researchers in their laboratories succumbed to the reality of funding imperatives, especially in high-tech fields such as nuclear physics, aerodynamics, and supercomputing that required expensive research equipment.

Furthermore, the intrusion of defense dollars into university budgets influenced institutional policies in ways that spread beyond individual faculties and laboratories holding contracts with the military. The National Defense Education Act of 1958, one of the many national responses to Sputnik, provided scholarship and fellowship support for students working in scientific and technical fields valued by the military. Faculties grew because many members taught reduced teaching loads, bought out of the classroom by research support from the Department of Defense. As universities added teaching faculty and made additional research appointments funded by government contracts, support infrastructure grew up around them—offices, services, parking spaces, etc. New research facilities were built at government expense and added to the universities' physical plant, requiring maintenance and still more support staff. Only annual infusions of funds from the Department of Defense could support this vast infrastructure. In 1984, 36 percent of MIT's engineering research budget came from the Department of Defense, as did 71 percent of the funding for the Laboratory for Computer Science, 62 percent for the Artificial Intelligence Laboratory, and 40 percent for the Research Laboratory of Electronics.[70]

The military presence in the academic community entailed more than financial dependency. Secrecy visited the university campus as a condition of government largess. Military research essential to national security naturally came under the strictures of government classification, an abused if necessary system that allowed government bureaucrats to restrict the flow of information. Most academics recognized a certain amount of confidentially in their work; for many, priority of publication was the currency of professional advancement and they accepted the need to keep their preliminary results confidential. But publishing was always the goal. Their findings did them no good until they appeared in print, preferably in prestigious, refereed journals. Military work, however, might never see the light of day. The more critical it was to the military services, the less likely it would be cleared for publication. Scientists who accepted these constraints could find themselves cut off from the normal round of papers, conferences, and published literature. Instead, they communed with other defense contractors and shared their research results with the services sponsoring their work.

During the Vietnam era, the issue of secrecy achieved an exceptional political salience on university campuses. At Stanford, for example, the dean of engineering announced in 1969 that the school would no longer accept classified contracts. The academic senate went one better by effectively banning all classified research from campus. The following month the trustees announced that the university would divest itself of the Stanford Research Institute (SRI), which had been incorporated in 1946 to promote research and education at Stanford; by 1969, most of SRI's funding was coming from the Department of Defense.[71] These responses to student and faculty protests had serious consequences for those scientists and engineers whose regular research agendas relied heavily on defense dollars. Laboratories, research associates, and graduate students were often dependent on continuation of that funding. Without it, the faculty would have to change fields or change institutions. In the end, the political pressure subsided at Stanford, and the restrictions on classified work slackened. But the fundamental incompatibility of secret research and academic ethos had been dramatically demonstrated. Similar struggles occurred on other campuses around the country.

As the pressures of the Cold War abated in the 1970s and 1980s, institutional prohibitions against defense funding subsided as well, even as a new and pernicious phenomenon crept onto campuses and research establishments around the country. The blurring of distinctions between military and civilian technologies, the embrace of dual-use technologies, and the growing overlap between military and economic security prompted the government to expand the scope of its classification schemes. The identification of military critical technologies in the 1980s and the spread of this categorization to other branches of government coincided with the Reagan administration's crackdown on technology transfer. After the worst instances of this government intrusion into academic life in the early 1980s, compromises were negotiated to balance the researcher's right to publish against the government's right to restrict the flow of information crucial to national security. But the experience suggests that the military/academic confrontations of the Vietnam era had not entirely dissipated.

More troubling still to many civilian scientists and engineers were the moral implications of research in the service of the military-industrial complex. Even before the complex took shape, the atomic bomb alerted many scholars and academics to the potential militarization of their professions. In 1946, veterans of the World War II Manhattan Project began publishing the *Bulletin of the Atomic Scientists*, with its ominous doomsday clock on the cover, warning of imminent nuclear cataclysm. Manhattan Project veterans also founded the Federation of Atomic Scientists in 1945; now the Federation of American Scientists, the group monitors science, technology, and public policy. In 1957, twenty-two scientists from ten countries met in Pugwash, Nova Scotia, to discuss the threat posed by nuclear weapons. Since then, hundreds of Pugwash conferences, symposia, and workshops have brought together scholars and public figures to address the world's problems, most of them tied to military science and technology; in 1995, the Pugwash conferences and their president, Joseph Rotblat, shared the Nobel Peace Prize. The Union of Concerned Scientists was founded in 1969 by a group of students and faculty at MIT to advocate scientific research on social and environmental problems instead of military programs. Computer Professionals for Social Responsibility (CPSR) formed in the late 1970s and crusaded through much of the 1980s against the automation of warfare, the loss of human agency inherent in the increasing use of computers for command and control of weapons of mass destruction. Computers, CPSR members believed, lent themselves to a kind of technological determinism, in which machines might one day decide what Jonathan Schell called "the fate of the earth."[72] CPSR advocated that its members refrain from working on Defense Department projects or accepting military funding.

A claim of guild privilege colored all such movements, but usually they were couched in moral terms. Scientists and engineers, they asserted, had a contract with society to use their special talents for the good of humanity. Science and technology should be bent to human purposes, to the amelioration of the human condition, not to instruments of oppression and destruction. While many citizens, including scientists and engineers, saw military arms and equipment as guarantors of national security and bulwarks against communist aggression, the protestors focused on the excesses of the military-industrial complex, believing that it posed a greater threat to the nation than the remote Soviets and their fellow travelers in Europe, Asia, Africa, and Latin America. The American experience in Vietnam fueled the perception that the vast arsenal of the Cold War was a blunt tool, one that the military could not be trusted to use wisely and humanely. This argument originated on American campuses and resonated there more deeply than in the country at large.

Some scientists and engineers, far from renouncing the military-industrial complex, warmly embraced it. Charles Stark Draper, for example, actively defended the military work of his Instrumentation Laboratory to his MIT colleagues and students. Edward Teller was perhaps the most strident and influential of these cold warriors. A co-developer of the U.S. hydrogen bomb, he played a notorious role in the revocation of Robert Oppenheimer's security clearance. Throughout the 1960s and 1970s he applied his considerable scientific talents to demonstrating that no nuclear test-ban treaty with the Soviet Union could be verified. In the 1980s, he helped convince President Reagan to launch the Strategic Defense Initiative (SDI). When American scientist Harrison Brown was negotiating with his Soviet counterparts in 1960 to organize a conference on the nuclear arms race, a Soviet spokesman said to him, "If you bring your Teller, we will bring ours."[73] Eisenhower may have had Teller in mind when he warned of a "scientific-technical elite."

In general, scientists and engineers lent themselves readily to the military-industrial complex. While some eschewed military research, many others embraced it as patriotic and stimulating. Most, no doubt, simply looked upon it as a source of patronage. Researchers are always engaged in an evolving negotiation with their patrons, seeking a balance between their own muses and the interests of those who pay the bills. In this sense, patrons always influence the research agendas of the societies they inhabit. For better or worse, the Department of Defense was the largest single patron of science and technology in the Cold War.

6

SOCIETY AND TECHNOLOGY

The Cold War imposed a unique and perverse logic, not just on strategists, but on the public at large.[74] The superpowers and the countries of the northern hemisphere living in the path of the radioactive fallout that would flood the atmosphere after release of the great nuclear arsenals rested precariously on what defense intellectual Albert Wohlstetter called a "delicate balance of terror."[75] Security was achieved only through mutual vulnerability. The prospect of mutual assured destruction chastened both sides to avoid armed confrontation at all costs. When such a confrontation arose in the Cuban Missile Crisis of 1962, the experience was so alarming that both superpowers worked consistently thereafter for détente. Each came to realize that its safety was hostage to its enemy's safety.

In such an atmosphere, the normal rules of diplomacy and war were stood on their head. The secrecy surrounding weapons systems was oppressive, yet both sides regularly leaked information to the other; it was essential, after all, that the other side knew and appreciated its enemy's capabilities, the range of its bombers, the accuracy of its missiles, the stealth of its submarines. Promoters of peace advocated the elimination of nuclear weapons, even though the peace itself was a product of those weapons. Both sides welcomed the intrusion of reconnaissance satellites, which gave each the assurance that the other was not mobilizing its forces, but for many years the United States insisted that it did not use these satellites.

The convoluted logic of this dance of death became famously public in the controversy over missile basing in the 1970s and 1980s. The improvement of American missile accuracy had prompted the Soviets to increase both the numbers and accuracy of their missiles, raising in Americans the like fear of an enemy first strike. One way to protect the American MX missile from a preemptive strike was to put each missile on a mobile carrier that would move over a closed course visiting twenty-three different shelters. The Soviets would never know which shelter housed a missile or if the missile was still on the carrier. But the placement of the missiles could not be allowed to violate the Strategic Arms Limitation Talks treaties of the 1970s, which had limited the allowable number of readily observable weapons. So the United States would load the carrier with the top open in full view of Soviet reconnaissance satellites. Furthermore, each shelter had viewing ports which would be opened to Soviet observation periodically or on challenge, to ensure that no more than one missile moved around each course. In a kind of strategic shell game, one side would lift the shell from time to time to let the other count the peas.[76]

Nowhere was the perversity of this relationship more compelling than in the race to build more and better strategic weapons. Perception was everything. It mattered not what a strategic arsenal could really do, only what the enemy thought it could do. Each side had to ensure that its enemy feared overkill, feared that its opponent's arsenal was powerful enough to destroy it several times over. Such an environment built irresistible pressure to err on the side of destruction. No calculus could allow the enemy to believe that he could launch a first strike and survive retaliation from the residue of his enemy's forces. So both sides built ever more warheads, ever more delivery systems. The largest missiles mounted multiple warheads, ensuring that some bombs from each carrier would reach their targets. In time, the multiple warheads were made to navigate independently to their respective targets. They could even maneuver in the face of enemy defenses, though such defenses posed little threat to their flight. At the peak, the two sides brandished more than 11,000 strategic warheads each, even though Defense Secretary Robert McNamara had concluded in the 1960s that 1,000 were enough to destroy the Soviet Union as a viable political and social entity. Not for nothing was the strategy called MAD.

The strategic arms race reached a climax in President Ronald Reagan's SDI, quickly dubbed "Star Wars" after a popular science-fiction movie. Convinced by a small coterie of advisors that technology could protect the United States from the MADness into which technology had cast the world, President Reagan proposed a layered defense system that would surround the United States with an impenetrable barrier against intercontinental ballistic missiles. Most informed observers in the United States and the Soviet Union realized that such a defense was beyond the current and foreseeable technical capability of even the United States. Again, however, perception trumped reality in the Alice-in-Wonderland

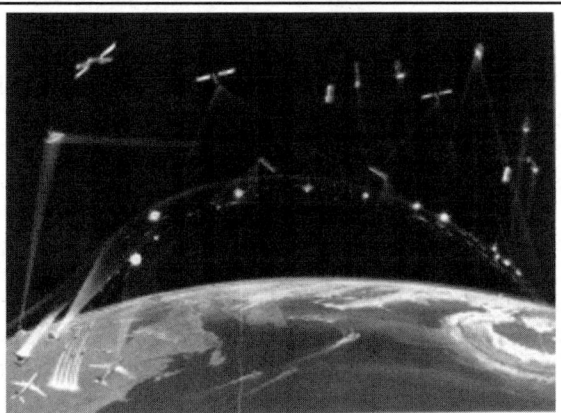

Figure 9. *On March 23, 1983, President Ronald Reagan proposed the Strategic Defense Initiative to make the United States invulnerable to attack by intercontinental ballistic missiles. It featured a "multilayer" defense against missile attack, intercepting missiles and their warheads throughout their flight. No technology then, or at any time in the twentieth century, proved even remotely capable of offering the protection President Reagan envisioned. But billions of dollars flowed annually into ballistic missile defense through the remainder of the century. (From* Strategic Defense Initiative: Progress and Promise *[Washington, D.C.: Department of Defense, 1989], p. 25.)*

world of Cold War logic. Many Americans embraced ballistic missile defense and kept the program going into the twenty-first century in spite of its failure to demonstrate a workable system. Not even the end of the Cold War arrested this development. Realizing that perception was everything, some opponents of SDI noted that it was fundamentally destabilizing, for if successful it would have deeply discounted the threat of the Soviet arsenal, tempting the Soviets to "use 'em or lose 'em." Advocates of SDI countered that by raising the ante in the research-and-development contest of the Cold War, SDI had forced the Soviets to admit the bankruptcy of their command economy and begin the transition that led to the collapse of the Soviet Union. Both arguments have merit; both reveal the centrality of technology in this complex calculus and the preeminence of perception. What observers thought about the technology was more important than the technology itself.

In such an atmosphere, it was easy to conjure an image of national leaders who had taken leave of their senses, one of the premises of director Stanley Kubrick's popular movie *Dr. Strangelove, or: How I Stopped Worrying and Learned to Love the Bomb*. In the memorable, climactic scene, Slim Pickens rides a huge phallic nuke to an orgasmic suicide symbolic of humanity's mad and self-destructive infatuation with these engines of destruction. Equally plausible was the suspicion that technology itself was in control. In the novel *Fail-safe* and its cinematic sequel, a U.S. bomber receives a false and irretrievable command to attack Moscow with its nuclear weapons. Not even Soviet-American cooperation can reverse the doomsday machine that has been set in motion.

The Cold War and its MAD arms race also contributed to the growth of an alarmist literature about technological determinism. Jacques Ellul launched the critique in 1964, claiming in *The Technological Society* that human agency was being lost to machines, which operated by a logic of their own.[77] In the United States, Lewis Mumford echoed this view in *The Myth of the Machine*, a two-volume assault on the military-industrial complex as a triumph of machine over human values.[78] In *Autonomous Technology: Technics Out of Control as a Theme in Political Thought*, Langdon Winner explored the roots of this notion in Western civilization, from Mary Shelley's *Frankenstein* to Kurt Vonnegut's *Player Piano*.[79] As with most critics of technological determinism, these scholars advocated a return of human agency, a conscious campaign to take control of our technology before it destroyed us. Their work, therefore, blended with one of the main themes of postmodernism and poststructuralism, the belief that Enlightenment rationalism had launched Western civilization on the path to an alarming modernity.

Other scholars sounded warnings more closely focused on the military-industrial complex. Paul Forman and others lamented the opportunity costs of the Cold War.[80] The billions of dollars invested in weapons research might have been better spent on medicine, social needs, agriculture, and other life-enhancing technologies. This proposition begged the question of whether or not defense funds were fungible; for example, would the superpowers have taxed themselves at the same rate and invested the funds more wisely had there been no Cold War?[81] Similarly, Paul Edwards argued that the computer, one of the core technologies behind the rapid transformation of information and communications at the turn of the twenty-first century, was shaped irreversibly by the military sponsorship that effected its early development. Because the military wanted computers and networks for command and control, they created a "closed world" in which the technology has those goals and values imbedded in its most fundamental structure. The chaotic riot of the Internet bears little resemblance to the hierarchical infrastructure of military "C³I" (command, control, communication, and information), but the alarm engendered by the excesses of Cold War technology nevertheless provides fertile ground for such conjectures.

In the end, Americans learned to live with the strange paradox that the military-industrial complex saved and threatened life at the same time. Its strategic arsenal preserved the peace while threatening all life in the northern hemisphere. Its conventional arms achieved troubling effectiveness in the Iraqi desert during the Gulf War, even while it kept American servicemen out of harm's way in Kosovo. U.S. military technology failed in Vietnam, in part because the enemy used terrain, tactics, and techniques against which its force was blunted. But out of the frustration of Vietnam came the smart weapons that set the world standard in the late twentieth century.

Americans also learned to live with fear. In the 1950s and early 1960s, when nuclear war seemed inevitable, children practiced hiding under their school desks in the event of nuclear attack, and prosperous citizens built bomb shelters in the curious faith that they would want to live in the wasteland left behind by nuclear war. The terrifying devastation of Hiroshima and Nagasaki was compounded by the unfolding nightmare of radiation effects on the survivors. Nuclear technology was at once our greatest achievement and our worst peril. Fear of nuclear weapons was projected onto commercial nuclear power, burdening utilities with litigation, safety, and decommissioning costs that far outweighed the economic benefits. The same fear contributed to the early retirement of the nuclear-powered commercial ship *Savannah*. In time, when nuclear war did not come, and when nuclear power plants did not melt down, the fear subsided. But each time a new state joined the nuclear club, as China did, for example, in 1964, and each time a nuclear power plant experienced a serious "excursion," as Three Mile Island did in the United States in 1979 and Chernobyl did in the Soviet Union in 1986, the old fear revived. In no other technology was the military-industrial complex's power to simultaneously protect and threaten so vividly and poignantly manifest.

While living with this fear, Americans also availed themselves of the cornucopia of technology spun off by the military-industrial complex. The aerospace industry rode defense dollars to world preeminence. Consumer electronics exploited the solid-state devices first developed for weapons and space applications. Major corporations such as General Electric, Motorola, and IBM kept one foot in the military marketplace and one in the civilian, finding cross-fertilizations that advanced technology in both. The Jeep, workhorse of World War II personal transportation, found itself transformed into a hot commercial product for upscale adventurers. Its distant successor, the army's HUMMWV (High Mobility Multi-purpose Wheeled Vehicle), became a status symbol for those with $70,000 or more to invest in an automobile wider than many parking spaces. By the end of the twentieth century, the military's global positioning satellite system was guiding everything from commercial ships and airliners to private yachtsmen and hunters and even drivers of Cadillacs equipped with the company's "NorthStar" system. Computer speech-recognition programs developed for the military found their way into interactive weather reports on the telephone, airline reservation systems, and even hotel guides to restaurants and other local businesses. For better or for worse, the products of the military-industrial complex found their way into almost every corner of modern life, to be welcomed openly, if often unknowingly, even by those who once took President Eisenhower's warning as prophetic.

CONCLUSION

The military-industrial complex in the United States took shape in the 1950s and 1960s and became politically salient in the Vietnam era. Thereafter it attracted less scholarly attention, even though it continued to pose a serious danger to the Republic, at least through the Reagan defense buildup of the early 1980s. American defense spending peaked in 1986 and declined steadily thereafter for the remainder of the twentieth century.[82] The military-industrial complex did not go away, nor did it cease to influence U.S. national policy. But its impact clearly subsided.

That impact must be weighed against the effect of comparable phenomenon in other countries and the impact of other special-interest groups in the United States. The other great military-industrial-political labyrinth of the Cold War, of course, arose in the Soviet Union. There, the ultimate "command economy" directed 10 percent to 20 percent of GDP to military purposes, roughly twice the percentage invested by the United States.[83] Military officers and directors of state-run industries and research institutions served in the Communist Party and sat in the Politburo. In retrospect it appears that the Soviets owed their remarkable achievements in military and space technology to a concentration of resources in these fields at the expense of domestic, civilian technology. One has only to look at their supersonic transport, their space shuttle, and their variable-sweep-wing aircraft to appreciate the extent to which they also relied upon imitation, if not outright theft, of Western technology. Still, their military-industrial-political network rivaled that of the United States and finally succumbed to the danger that Eisenhower had perceived: it was possible to bankrupt the state by subordinating sound economic growth to military imperatives.

At the other end of the spectrum, Japan, alone among the great industrial powers, created virtually no military-industrial complex during the Cold War. Constrained by the terms of the peace treaty ending World War II, Japan relied upon the United States for its strategic security and maintained only local defense forces, which were precluded from operating overseas. It nonetheless developed a kind of command economy in which the government intervened aggressively in a nominally free market to promote industries and technologies deemed to be in the national interest. The primary instrument of this policy was the Ministry of International Trade and Industry. While most of this intervention occurred in consumer industries such as electronics and automobiles, Japan also supported such military-related fields as spaceflight, shipbuilding, and computers. Though Japan was often accused of a kind of economic imperialism, its particular version of statist capitalism never found itself tainted with the moral and ideological opprobrium that attached to the military-industrial complex in the United States.

Other industrialized states also wrestled with the tension between national security and free-market capitalism. Many U.S. allies within NATO struggled to develop aircraft, ships, and spacecraft that could both meet the country's individual and alliance needs and also find a niche in the lucrative international arms market. For most, competition with the United States presented formidable hurdles, leading, for example, to the 1965 cancellation of Britain's Tactical/Strike Reconnaissance 2 aircraft. NATO negotiated some cooperative agreements to purchase arms and equipment outside the United States, but seldom the expensive, major weapons systems that were the hallmark of the American military-industrial complex. And from time to time the Americans purchased a major piece of military equipment abroad, as the Marines did in taking on Britain's Harrier vertical take-off and landing fighter/attack aircraft. Some countries outside the major alliances, such as Sweden and Israel, developed military technologies for their own use and for international sales, without, however, building up infrastructures that would warrant the label military-industrial complex.

The general decline in world military spending, beginning in 1987, and the end of the Cold War in 1991, were both reflected in a shrinking American military budget. By the end of the twentieth century, defense spending in the United States accounted for 34 percent of the world's total, but consumed less than 4 percent of gross domestic product. By and large, the list of leading defense contractors continued throughout the Cold War to map well on the *Fortune* 500 list, as it had in 1958. Defense was still big business in the United States at the end of the twentieth century, but it did not continue to swell in size and influence as Eisenhower had anticipated in the 1950s.

This is not to say that Eisenhower's warning could be forgotten. Many of the abuses and dangers first apparent in the 1950s were still extant in 1999, sanctioned now by tradition and long practice. Ballistic missile defense continued to absorb billions of dollars every year in spite of the end of the Cold War and the failure to produce a workable system; it was the 1990s version of the B-1 bomber. The defense "draw-down" of the 1990s prompted the Department of Defense to subsidize mergers of consolidation within the defense industry. In 1993, for example, Martin Marietta Chairman Norman Augustine proposed a merger with fellow aerospace industry giant Lockheed. Defense officials William Perry and John Deutch requested and received conflict-of-interest waivers to approve Augustine's plan—both had consulted for him at Martin Marietta before joining the Clinton administration—and then oversaw an $855 million subsidy to their former employer, including $31 million in bonuses to officials at the two companies. Augustine alone received $8.2 million. The new company, Lockheed Martin, quickly put out a brochure boasting that it had "facilities in all 50 states." In 1997, the new company gave $667,000 in political contributions to both parties, part of the $2.5 million contributed by the seven largest defense contractors.[84]

Whatever the merits or deficiencies of Defense Department policy toward the Lockheed/Martin Marietta merger, it surely had the appearance of the same impropriety that gave the military-industrial complex its dark reputation. Yet, in the late 1990s, the behavior seemed less exceptional than it did to Eisenhower in the 1950s. Government support of large-scale commercial technologies in fields ranging from the supersonic transport and the space shuttle to the Clinch River Breeder Reactor and synthetic fuels revealed similar patterns.[85] Cost overruns, poor performance, cooptation of congressmen, buying in, and political inertia appear to be systemic risks in all such developments. So too is the temptation to shape national policy by representing these projects as essential to national security and well-being. The supersonic transport would ensure the competitive advantage of the U.S. aerospace industry and its commercial airlines. The space shuttle would keep the United States ahead of the Soviet Union. The breeder reactor and the synthetic fuels program would protect the country from the machinations of the international oil cartel. Even the use of political contributions, the new currency of political leverage in the late twentieth century, crept into some of these programs.

What, then, might be said about the five areas in which the military-industrial complex exerted its greatest influence?

The impact on civil-military relations turned out to be less than Harold Lasswell had once feared. In 1965, Lasswell revisited his thesis about the garrison state.[86] Though the United States was in the grips of the Vietnam conflict, with countless military-industrial scandals still in train, Lasswell concluded that the country had not become a garrison state. The Soviet Union had; the United States had not—yet. Had Lasswell returned at the end of the twentieth century to reprise his analysis, it seems doubtful that he would have changed his mind. Nor would President Eisenhower have found the militarized society he warned against. The worst excesses of the complex had subsided as the country moved from confrontation to détente, as reforms and whistle-blowers curbed the worst chicanery, and as the world turned from military rivalry among the great powers to economic competition. The distinctions between civilian and military blurred, but the constitutional order persisted.[87]

Defense industries dealt with the government differently in 1999 than they had in 1948. The revolving door of industry/government employment continued to turn, weaving a "thick fabric" of cooperation and conflict of interest. Subcontracting remained a political as well as a business tool, creating jobs in the districts of congressmen who would vote on defense programs. Like the Department of Defense, industry looked for dual-use technologies that would sell in both military and civilian markets. And technologies developed with defense funding were spun off whenever possible into civilian applications. But because reforms in federal contracting usually applied to military and civilian agencies alike, government relations with the defense industry came to look more like other industrial relations than they had in the Eisenhower administration.

Scientists and engineers at the end of the twentieth century continued to work under military sponsorship. Most academic institutions developed regulations for the conduct of classified research that allowed this work to continue on campus. The protests and opprobrium that attached to this funding in the Vietnam era abated. For most of the Cold War, the Department of Defense was the largest single patron of research and development. It shaped not only the agenda of American science and technology but also the process by which they were conducted. Scientists and engineers were not simply passive beneficiaries of this largesse; they participated in the battle of the experts that shaped policies ranging from the national research agenda to arms control. No doubt that research agenda differed from what it might have been, absent the Cold War. But, at the end of the twentieth century, the country's scientific and technological landscape more closely resembled Japan's, where military budgets were constrained throughout the Cold War, than it did Russia's, where exceptional percentages of GDP flowed into military research and development.

Government departments participated variously in the Cold War race for superior technology. On the leading edge, closely aligned with the Department of Defense, were the weapons branches of the Department of Energy (and its predecessors) and the intelligence agencies—the CIA, NRO, NSA, DIA, etc. At the other end of the spectrum were those arms of government focused primarily on the promotion of science and technology for domestic purposes—the National Institutes of Health, for example, and the Department of Agriculture. In between, many agencies found themselves engaged with the military-industrial complex. NASA, for example, built its manned space program around a race with the Soviet Union that was a continuation of the Cold War by other means. Its budget fell steadily after the Apollo program as that competition waned. In contrast, the Environmental Protection Agency saw its responsibilities grow as the sorry environmental record of the country's military bases and weapons laboratories came to light. Those agencies of government having no contact with the military-industrial complex were a small minority.

Finally, public alarm over the military-industrial complex appears to have subsided after the 1970s. The end of the Cold War and the reduction of the world's nuclear stockpiles reduced the apocalyptic fears once conjured by the icon of the mushroom cloud. The number of nuclear weapons and the world total of world military spending declined from the late 1980s through the end of the century. While the lessening of public concern failed to stimulate a revival of support for commercial nuclear power, it did seem to accompany a growing appreciation of military technology. If the United States could employ high-technology to limit both its own casualties and collateral casualties in its military engagements, then this was all to the good. *Dr. Strangelove* receded in the public imagination, replaced to some extent by the anonymous wizards whose technological marvels brought American troops through the intervention in Kosovo without a combat fatality.

The military-industrial complex, therefore, appears more normal than it did in the early years of the Cold War. It was the mechanism by which the United States chose to promote a certain kind of scientific and technological development. It produced marvels ranging from stealth aircraft to multi-sensor reconnaissance satellites. It spun off technologies that range from the Internet to global positioning satellites. Whether or not science and technology would have advanced differently or more beneficially without this patronage one can only guess. It becomes increasingly difficult, however, to see that it produced the militarized state about which Harold Lasswell and Dwight Eisenhower once worried. It is probably more accurate to say that the centrality of science and technology to modern life, and the continuing importance of military preparedness to U.S. security, probably insure that soldiers, scientists, and engineers will continue to be part of C. Wright Mills's power elite.

NOTES

1. A similar set of relationships organizes the discussion of Harvey M. Sapolsky, Eugene Gholz, and Allen Kaufman, "Security Lessons from the Cold War," *Foreign Affairs* 78 (July/August 1999): 77–89.

2. Stanley Baumgartner does not even believe that "military-industrial complex" is an appropriate description for an essentially positive phenomenon; see his *The Lonely Warriors: Case for the Military-Industrial Complex* (Los Angeles: Nash Pub., 1970). The great majority of scholarly opinion, however, disagrees. See, for example, Sidney Lens, *The Military-Industrial Complex* (Philadelphia: Pilgrim Press, 1970); Carroll W. Pursell, comp., *The Military-Industrial Complex* (New York: Harper & Row, 1972). The most balanced account is Steven Rosen, comp., *Testing the Theory of the Military-Industrial Complex* (Lexington, Mass.: Lexington Books, 1973).

3. The $1 billion figure comes from Elsbeth E. Freudenthal, *The Aviation Business: From Kitty Hawk to Wall Street* (New York: Vanguard Press, 1940), 35–61. I. B. Holley reports the delivery of aircraft in *Ideas and Weapons: Exploitation of the Aerial Weapon by the United States during World War I; A Study in the Relationship of Technological Advance, Military Doctrine, and the Development of Weapons* (New Haven, Conn.: Yale University Press, 1953), 106, 131–32.

4. Andrew Gibson and Arthur Donovan, *The Abandoned Ocean: A History of United States Maritime Policy* (Columbia: University of South Carolina Press, 2000), 112–15.

5. Stuart D. Brandes, *Warhogs: A History of War Profits in America* (Lexington: University Press of Kentucky, 1997).

6. Stephen J. Zempolich, "Dwight David Eisenhower and the Military-Industrial Complex: Advocacy to Opposition, 1928–1961," Senior Honors Thesis, Duke University, 1985.

7. Eisenhower appears to have had in mind what Herbert Hoover called an "associative state." See Ellis Hawley, "Herbert Hoover, the Commerce Secretariat and the Vision of an 'Associative State,' 1921–1928," *Journal of American History* 41 (June 1947): 116–40.

8. John U. Nef, *War and Human Progress: An Essay on the Rise of Industrial Civilization* (Cambridge, Mass.: Harvard University Press, 1950).

9. Alex Roland, *Underwater Warfare in the Age of Sail* (Bloomington: Indiana University Press, 1978).

10. Elting Morison, *Men, Machines, and Modern Times* (Cambridge, Mass.: MIT Press, 1966), 17–44.

11. Some of these motives are explored in Michael Sherry, *Preparing for the Next War: American Plans for Postwar Defense, 1941–1945* (New Haven, Conn.: Yale University Press, 1977).

12. Richard V. Damms, "Containing the Military-Industrial-Congressional Complex: President Eisenhower's Science Advisers and the Case of the Nuclear-powered Aircraft," *Essays in Economic and Business History* 14 (1996): 279–89.

13. Stuart W. Leslie, *The Cold War and American Science: The Military-Industrial-Academic Complex at MIT and Stanford* (New York: Columbia University Press, 1993); Rebecca S. Lowen, *Creating the Cold War University: The Transformation of Stanford* (Berkeley: University of California Press, 1997).

14. C. Wright Mills, *The Power Elite* (New York: Oxford University Press, 1956).

15. Eisenhower was also alarmed and frustrated by the efforts of physicist Edward Teller and other opponents of arms control, who used scientific arguments to block a partial nuclear test ban agreement with the Soviet Union.

16. As this literature appeared in the 1970s, Robert D. Cuff observed that it was "an intensely ideological body of work." See his "An Organizational Perspective on the Military-Industrial Complex," *Business History Review* 52 (summer 1978): 251.

17. Richard Cowen, "Iron and an Early Military-Industrial Complex," chap. 10 in *History of Life* (New York: McGraw Hill, 1976).

18. Paul A. C. Koistinen, *The Military-Industrial Complex: A Historical Perspective* (New York: Praeger, 1980). See the same author's trilogy: *Beating Plowshares into Swords: The Political Economy of American Warfare, 1606–1865*; *Mobilizing for Modern War: The Political Economy of American Warfare, 1865–1919*; and *Planning War, Pursuing Peace: The Political Economy of American Warfare, 1920–1939* (Lawrence: University Press of Kansas, 1996, 1997, 1998). See also Franklin Cooling, *Gray Steel and Blue Water Navy: The Formative Years of America's Military-Industrial Complex* (Hamden, Conn.: Archon Books, 1979).

19. William H. McNeill, *The Pursuit of Power: Technology, Armed Force, and Society since A.D. 1000* (Chicago: University of Chicago Press, 1982), 269–85.

20. C. Vann Woodward, "The Age of Reinterpretation," *American Historical Review* 66 (1960): 1–19.

21. Michael H. Armacost, *The Politics of Weapons Innovation: The Thor-Jupiter Controversy* (New York: Columbia University Press, 1969).

22. George A. Reed, "U.S. Defense Policy, U.S. Air Force Doctrine, and Strategic Nuclear Weapon Systems, 1958–1964: The Case of the Minuteman ICBM," PhD dissertation, Duke University, 1986.

23. *Project Horizon: A U.S. Army Study for the Establishment of a Lunar Military Outpost*, 2 vols. (Washington, D.C.: U.S. Army, 1959).

24. Or at least so says the published data. If the black budget for reconnaissance and other secret programs were added, along with NASA subsidization of air force shuttle missions, the balance would shift significantly.

25. Alain C. Enthoven and K. Wayne Smith, *How Much Is Enough? Shaping the Defense Program, 1961–1969* (New York: Harper & Row, 1971).

26. Robert R. Bowie and Richard H. Immerman, *Waging Peace: How Eisenhower Shaped an Enduring Cold War Strategy* (New York: Oxford University Press, 1998), esp. 75, 96–108.

27. Charts 1–4 were created from a variety of sources. Information on the Gross Domestic Product comes from *National Income and Product Accounts of the United States, 1929–94*, vol. 1 (Washington, D.C.: Department of Commerce, 1998); and *Statistical Abstract of the United States,* 118th ed. (Washington, D.C.: Department

of Commerce, 1998). Data on total federal outlays and total military spending comes from *Budget of the United States Government, Fiscal Year 2000: Historical Tables* (Washington, D.C.: Office of Management and Budget, 1999). Data on total government research comes from three sources: for 1948–51, U.S. National Science Foundation, *Annual Report* (Washington, D.C.: NSF, 1951); for 1952–66, National Science Foundation, *Federal Funds for Research, Development and Other Scientific Activities, Fiscal Years 1969, 1970, 1971*, Surveys of Science Resource Series, NSF 70–38, vol. 19 (Washington, D.C.: NSF, 1971); for 1967–95, National Science Foundation, *Federal Funds Survey, Detailed Historical Tables, Fiscal Years 1951–1997*, at http://www.nsf.gov/sbe/srs/fedfnd45/hist45/pdfstart.htm, 6 March 2000. Data on military research and development for the period 1945–51, which includes expenditures for the Manhattan Project, 1945–47, is from National Science Foundation, *Annual Report* for 1951 (cited above); for 1952–66, *Federal Funds for Research, Development, and Other Scientific Activities, Fiscal Years 1971, 1972, 1973,* Surveys of Science Resource Series, vol. 21 (Washington, D.C.: NSF, 1973); and for 1967–95, *Federal Funds Survey* (cited above).

28. "The Fortune Directory: The 500 Largest U.S. Industrial Corporations," *Fortune,* July 1959, 12–16; William Proxmire, "Retired High-Ranking Military Officers," in Pursell, *Military-Industrial Complex,* 260–62.

29. H. L. Nieburg, *In the Name of Science* (Chicago: Quadrangle Books, 1966), 184–99.

30. Seymour Melman, *Pentagon Capitalism: The Political Economy of War* (New York: McGraw-Hill, 1970), 227.

31. Nick Kotz, *Wild Blue Yonder: Money, Politics, and the B-1 Bomber* (New York: Pantheon Books, 1988).

32. Arnold Levine, *Managing NASA in the Apollo Era*, NASA SP-4102 (Washington, D.C.: NASA, 1982), 155.

33. Alex Roland, "The Shuttle: Triumph or Turkey?" *Discover* 6 (November 1985): 29–49.

34. Michael Sherry argues that it did in *In the Shadow of War: The United States since the 1930s* (New Haven, Conn.: Yale University Press, 1995).

35. Harold Lasswell, "The Garrison State," *The American Journal of Sociology* 46 (January 1941): 455–68; reprinted in *Essays on the Garrison State,* ed. Jay Stanley (New Brunswick, N.J.: Transaction Publishers, 1997), 55–75.

36. Lasswell, "The Garrison State," in *Essays on the Garrison State,* 59–60.

37. Eisenhower said in a press conference on 11 March 1959 that continuing increases in defense spending threatened to drive the United States into a "garrison state." *Public Papers of the Presidents of the United States: Dwight D. Eisenhower, 1960–61* (Washington, D.C.: GPO, 1961), 250.

38. James Barron, "High Cost of Military Parts," *New York Times,* 1 September 1983, 1; and Mark Thompson, "Pliers Cost $999; New Spending Probe Urged," *The Record* (Washington, D.C.), 20 June 1990, A01. For a thoughtful discussion of such overruns, see Jacques Gansler, *Affording Defense* (Cambridge, Mass.: MIT Press, 1991), 195–207.

39. Samuel P. Huntington, *The Soldier and the State: The Theory and Politics of Civil-Military Relations* (Cambridge, Mass.: Belknap Press of Harvard University Press, 1957).

40. James Fallows, *National Defense* (New York: Random House, 1981), 10.

41. Robert H. Johnson, *Improbable Dangers: U.S. Conceptions of Threat in the Cold War and After* (New York: St. Martin's, 1997).

42. Robert F. Coulam, *The Illusion of Choice: Problems in the Development of F-111 Fighter-Bomber*, Teaching and Research Materials, No. 14 (Cambridge, Mass.: Public Policy Program, John F. Kennedy School of Government, 1973), 180–83.

43. Robert J. Art, *The TFX Decision: McNamara and the Military* (Boston: Little, Brown, 1968), 44.

44. Donald MacKenzie, *Inventing Accuracy: An Historical Sociology of Nuclear Missile Guidance* (Cambridge, Mass.: MIT Press, 1990).

45. Quoted in "The Military Critical Technologies List," ADA-146 998 (Washington, D.C.: Office of the Under Secretary of Defense Research and Engineering, 1984), 1.

46. "The Military Critical Technologies List," A-i.

47. Department of Defense, "Critical Technologies Plan," for the Committees on Armed Services, United States Congress, AD-A234 900, May 1991, quote at p. II-5.

48. Herbert N. Foerstel, *Secret Science: Federal Control of American Science and Technology* (Westport, Conn.: Praeger, 1993).

49. "Secrecy in University-Based Research: Who Controls? Who Tells?" special issue of *Science, Technology, and Human Values* 10 (spring 1982).

50. Daniel Patrick Moynihan, *Secrecy: The American Experience* (New Haven, Conn.: Yale University Press, 1998).

51. Foerstel, *Secret Science*, 13

52. "National Critical Technologies List," Appendix A, http://www.whitehouse. gov/WH/EOP/OSTP/CTIformatted/AppA/appa.html, 7 March 2000, 1.

53. Harvey M. Sapolsky, *The Polaris System Development: Bureaucratic and Programmatic Success in Government* (Cambridge, Mass.: Harvard University Press, 1972).

54. John Clayton Lonnquest, "The Face of Atlas: General Bernard Schriever and the Development of the Atlas Intercontinental Ballistic Missile, 1953–1960," PhD dissertation, Duke University, 1996.

55. Merritt Roe Smith, *Harpers Ferry Armory and the New Technology: The Challenge of Change* (Ithaca, N.Y.: Cornell University Press, 1977).

56. David Hounshell, *From the American System to Mass Production, 1800–1932: The Development of Manufacturing Technology in the United States* (Baltimore, Md.: Johns Hopkins University Press, 1984).

57. Lonnquest, "The Face of Atlas," 92. The following account is drawn from Lonnquest and from H. L. Nieburg, *In the Name of Science* (Chicago: Quadrangle Books, 1966), 200–17.

58. Berkeley Rice, *The C-5A Scandal: An Inside Story of the Military-Industrial Complex* (Boston: Houghton Mifflin, 1971), 15–16. The following account of the C-5A is based on this source.

59. Anthony Sampson, *The Arms Bazaar: The Companies, the Dealers, the Bribes: From Vickers to Lockheed* (London: Hodder and Stoughton, 1977).

60. Jonathan Turley, quoted in David Armstrong, "The Nation's Dirty, Big Secret," *Boston Globe*, 14 November 1999.

61. John Ferris offers an informed and critical appraisal of the literature on intelligence in "Coming in from the Cold War: The Historiography of American Intelligence, 1945–1990," *Diplomatic History* 1 (1995): 87–115.

62. William E. Burrows, *This New Ocean: The Story of the First Space Age* (New York: Random House, 1998), 528n.

63. Walter A. McDougall, *The Heavens and the Earth: A Political History of the Space Age* (New York: Basic Books, 1985).

64. *Public Papers of the President: Dwight D. Eisenhower, 1960* (Washington, D.C.: Government Printing Office, 1961), 1037.

65. Leslie, *Cold War and American Science*, 32–41, 90–99.

66. *The Top 200 Defense Contractors*, special issue of *Military Forum* 6 (August 1989): 67.

67. Leslie, *Cold War and American Science*, 63–75.

68. Paul Forman, "Behind Quantum Electronics: National Security as Basis for Physical Research in the United States, 1940–1960," *Historical Studies in the Physical Sciences* 18 (1987): 149–229; Paul Forman and José M. Sánchez-Ron, eds., *National Military Establishments and the Advancement of Science and Technology* (Dordrecht: Kluwer Academic Publishers, 1996), esp. 9–14, 261–326.

69. Paul Edwards, *The Closed World: Computers and the Politics of Discourse in Cold War America* (Cambridge, Mass.: MIT Press, 1996).

70. Leslie, *Cold War and American Science*, 252.

71. Leslie, *Cold War and American Science*, 243–47.

72. Jonathan Schell, *The Fate of the Earth* (New York: Knopf, 1982).

73. Quoted in Fred J. Cook, *The Warfare State* (New York: Macmillan, 1962), 243. See also William J. Broad, *Teller's War: The Top-Secret Story behind the Star Wars Deception* (New York: Simon & Schuster, 1992).

74. See Ann Douglas's thoughts on "cold-war speak" and other cultural features of the era in "Periodizing the American Century: Modernism, Postmodernism, and Postcolonialism in the Cold War Context," *Modernism/Modernity* 5 (1998): 71–98, quote at 79.

75. Albert Wohlstetter, "The Delicate Balance of Terror," *Foreign Affairs* 37 (January 1959): 211–34.

76. Mary Kaldor, *The Baroque Arsenal* (New York: Hill & Wang, 1981), 186–87.

77. Jacques Ellul, *The Technological Society* (New York: Vintage, 1964).

78. Lewis Mumford, *The Myth of the Machine*, 2 vols. (New York: Harcourt Brace Jovanovich, 1967–70).

79. Langdon Winner, *Autonomous Technology: Technics out of Control as a Theme in Political Thought* (Cambridge, Mass.: MIT Press, 1977).

80. See Forman, "Behind Quantum Electronics"; Forman and Sánchez-Ron, *National Military Establishments*; and Edwards, *The Closed World*. A serious attempt to count the cost of the U.S. nuclear arsenal appears in Stephen I. Scwhartz, ed., *Atomic Audit: The Costs and Consequences of U.S. Nuclear Weapons since 1940* (Washington, D.C.: Brookings Institution Press, 1998).

81. Paul Higgs argues that the military-industrial complex clearly shaped the American economy in the second half of the twentieth century, but he adds that economic historians need to learn more about its impact on "the rate and direction of technological change." See his "The Cold War Economy: Opportunity Costs, Ideology, and the Politics of Crisis," *Explorations in Economic History* 31 (1994): 283–312.

82. There was a slight increase in 1992 caused by the Gulf War, but most of that additional spending was recovered from America's allies after the war.

83. In the United States, the percent of GDP devoted to the defense during the Cold War peaked at 13.9 (1953) during the Korean War and subsided slowly thereafter. But it fell below 10 percent in 1956 and returned to that level only once thereafter (1958). Not even in the Vietnam era did defense spending rise to 10 percent of GDP. Attempts to estimate the "burden" of defense spending on the Soviet economy have proved vexing. See Noel E. Firth and James H. Noren, *Soviet Defense Spending: A History of CIA Estimates, 1950–1990* (College Station: Texas A & M University Press, 1998), esp. 128–39. The 10–20 percent range is reported by the International Institute for Strategic Studies, *The Military Balance* (London: IISS, 1984), 15.

84. http://www.foreignpolicy-infocus.org/papers/micr/fig_6.htm, 30 January 2000.

85. Linda R. Cohen and Roger G. Noll, *The Technology Pork Barrel* (Washington, D.C.: Brookings Institution, 1991).

86. Harold Lasswell, "The Garrison State Hypothesis Today [1962]," in Stanley, ed., Essays on the Garrison State, 77–116.

87. Peter D. Feaver and Richard H. Kohn, "Digest of Findings and Studies Presented at The Conference on the Military and Civilian Society, Cantigny Conference Center, 1st Division Museum, 28–29 October 1999," available at http://www.unc.edu/depts/tiss/CIVMIL.htm.

BIBLIOGRAPHIC ESSAY

The literature on the military-industrial complex is best approached chronologically. Begin with Dwight Eisenhower's farewell address, which introduced the term, in *Public Papers of the President of the United States: Dwight D. Eisenhower* (Washington, D.C.: General Printing Office, 1961), supplemented by Charles J. G. Griffin, "New Light on Eisenhower's Farewell Address," *Presidential Studies Quarterly* 22 (summer 1992): 469–79. Compare his formulation of the problem with C. Wright Mills, *The Power Elite* (New York: Oxford University Press, 1956) and the writings of Harold Lasswell on the garrison state; the latter are collected with an insightful appreciation by the editor in Harold Dwight Lasswell and Jay Stanley, *Essays on the Garrison State* (New Brunswick, N.J.: Transaction Publishers, 1997). The intent and object of Eisenhower's warning about a "scientific and technical elite" draws an entire chapter in science advisor George Kistiakowsky's *A Scientist at the White House: The Private Diary of President Eisenhower's Special Assistant for Science and Technology* (Cambridge, Mass.: Harvard University Press, 1976). The irony of Eisenhower's warning is explored in Stephen Zempolich, "Dwight David Eisenhower and the Military-Industrial Complex: Advocacy to Opposition, 1928–1961," Senior Honors Thesis, Duke University, 1985.

Only in the Vietnam era did the concept of a military-industrial complex achieve salience in the intellectual community. The most balanced and insightful appraisal is still Steven Rosen, comp., *Testing the Theory of the Military-Industrial Complex* (Lexington, Mass: Lexington Books, 1973), which treats the existence of the complex as a hypothesis. Carroll W. Pursell achieves something of the same detachment in *The Military-Industrial Complex* (New York: Harper & Row, 1972) by mixing primary sources with critical analyses. More typical of the Vietnam-era literature on the topic is William Proxmire, *Report from Wasteland: America's Military-Industrial Complex* (New York: Praeger, 1970).

Others conceptualize the problem in slightly different ways. Fred J. Cook envisions *The Warfare State* (New York: Macmillan, 1962). Michael Sherry argues in *In the Shadow of War: The United States since the 1930s* (New Haven, Conn.: Yale University Press, 1995) that the country succumbed to militarization in the Cold War. Physicist Ralph Lapp warns of *The Weapons Culture* (New York: W. W. Norton, 1968). Economist Seymour Melman believes that Robert McNamara had seized control of the levers of power and initiated a period of state control of the economy in what he called *Pentagon Capitalism: The Political Economy of War* (New York: McGraw-Hill, 1970). In a retrospective analysis, *In the Shadow of the Garrison State: America's Anti-Statism and Its Cold War Grand Strategy* (Princeton, N.J.: Princeton University Press, 2000), Aaron L. Friedberg concludes that anti-statist forces deeply rooted in American culture prevented it from the growth and concentration of power in the central government that the Soviet Union experienced. Walter McDougall's *The Heavens and the Earth: A*

Political History of the Space Age (New York: Basic Books, 1984) argues that the scientific-technological competition of the Cold War created a technocracy in the United States that rivaled that of the Soviet Union and exerted undue influence on national life. In *The Baroque Arsenal* (New York: Hill and Wang, 1981), Mary Kaldor argues that weapons systems had become an end in themselves, artifacts that failed to serve the purposes for which they were first invoked. Most of these scholars share a belief with President Eisenhower that the phenomenon endangered the republic. Many situate themselves in the "permanent adversarial culture" that historian Howard Zinn has seen emerging from the Vietnam War and civil rights movements (Howard Zinn, "The Politics of History in the Era of the Cold War: Repression and Resistance," in Noam Chomsky, et al., eds., *The Cold War and the University: Toward an Intellectual History of the Postwar Years* [New York: New Press, 1997], 35–72).

Attempts to historicize the military-industrial complex have demonstrated more balance and perspective. William McNeill uses the Anglo-German naval race preceding World War I to model the military-industrial complex in *The Pursuit of Power: Technology, Armed Force, and Society since A.D. 1000* (Chicago: University of Chicago Press, 1982). In *The Military-Industrial Complex: A Historical Perspective* (New York: Praeger, 1980) and in three subsequent volumes in the 1990s, Paul A. C. Koistinen examines the relationship between war and industry throughout American history. Benjamin Franklin Cooling achieves equal balance in *Gray Steel and Blue Water Navy: The Formative Years of America's Military-Industrial Complex, 1881–1917* (Hamden, Conn.: Archon Books, 1979) and in *War, Business, and American Society: Historical Perspectives on the Military-Industrial Complex* (Port Washington, N.Y.: Kennikat Press, 1977). Thomas P. Hughes examines three Cold War development projects—SAGE, Atlas, and ARPANET—in a meditation on large-scale technological systems in *Rescuing Prometheus* (New York: Pantheon, 1998). James Fallows, journalist and former speechwriter for President Jimmy Carter, uses his access, insight, and vantage point to see both the strengths and weaknesses of the American defense establishment in *National Defense* (New York: Random House, 1981).

Though many authors have come to see the military-industrial complex without the alarmist, jaundiced, and adversarial bias that marked much of the 1970s literature, few have essayed an outright defense of the phenomenon. John Stanley Baumgartner tries in *The Lonely Warriors: Case for the Military-Industrial Complex* (Los Angeles: Nash Pub., 1970). More surprisingly, several authors in Noam Chomsky et al., *The Cold War and the University* (New York: New Press, 1997) note some positive, if often unintentional, consequences of government support for academic research. Most notably, Harvard biologist R. C. Lewontin argues in "The Cold War and the Transformation of the Academy" (1–34) that massive infusions of government funding during and after World War II bred a healthy "socialization of intellectual work" that the United States had eschewed throughout its previous history. Government dollars gave academics stature and power that they had previously failed to achieve, both within their institutions and in society at large. He ignores or discounts the negative impact of this funding on universities and scientists laid out in works such as Stuart W. Leslie, *The Cold War and American Science: The Military-Industrial-Academic Complex at MIT and Stanford* (New York: Columbia University Press, 1993), and Paul Forman, "Behind Quantum Electronics: National Security as Basis for Physical Research in the United States, 1940–1960," *Historical Studies in the Physical Sciences* 18 (1987): 149–229.

For many authors the term "military-industrial complex" has become a neutral descriptor of the relationship that states establish between their security forces and the industry supplying them. For example, Masako Ikegami-Andersson lays out a theoretical taxonomy of these relationships in *The Military-Industrial Complex: The Cases of Sweden and Japan* (Aldershot/Brookfield, Mass.: Dartmouth, 1992). In *Innovation and the Arms Race: How the United States and the Soviet Union Develop New Military Technologies* (Ithaca, N.Y.: Cornell University Press, 1988), Matthew Evangelista demonstrates that the relationship between the military, the arms industry, and the state were very different in the Soviet Union and the United States. In the USSR, all three shared a common agenda, focus, and set of priorities. These findings are confirmed in David Holloway, *The Soviet Union and the Arms Race*, 2d ed. (New Haven, Conn.: Yale University Press, 1994). The USSR did not need a military-industrial complex, it was a military-industrial complex (Walter McDougall attributes this insight to his late political-scientist colleague at Berkeley, Paul Seabury. McDougall, "The Cold War Excursion of Science," *Diplomatic History* 24 [winter 2000]: 120). The defense industry always remained responsive to party control; it did not determine policy. See also Holloway's *Stalin and the Bomb: The Soviet Union and Atomic Energy, 1939–1956* (Ithaca, N.Y.: Cornell University Press, 1994), and Robert Perry's "American Styles of Military R&D" (89–112), one of many stimulating analyses in *The Genesis of New Weapons: Decision Making for Military R&D*, ed. Franklin A. Long and Judith Reppy (New York: Pergamon Press, 1980).

In the United States, the term "military-industrial complex" retains the pejorative flavor of the early Cold War. Critics such as World Watch's William D. Hartung, for example, believe that the military-industrial complex survived the Cold War and continues to shape U.S. policy. See his web page, "Military-Industrial Complex Revisited: How Weapons Makers are Shaping U.S. Foreign and Military Policies," at http://www.foreignpolicy-infocus.org/papers/micr/notes.html, 30 January 2000. Chalmers Johnson believes that the Pentagon has insulated itself against rational control by the political system and continues to spend at unnecessary levels; see his *Blowback: The Costs and Consequences of American Empire* (New York: Metropolitan Books, 2000). It is not clear, however, that the abuses cited by such critics differ in kind, or even in degree, from those in comparable civilian realms; see Linda R. Cohen and Roger G. Noll, *The Technology Pork Barrel* (Washington, D.C.: Brookings Institution, 1991). The military-industrial complex may be simply a special case of the corruption, waste, and mismanagement that seem to attend all large government programs.

A traditional attempt to see what Louis J. Halle called *The Cold War as History* (New York: Harper & Row, 1967) is John Lewis Gaddis, *We Now Know: Rethinking Cold War History* (New York: Oxford University Press, 1997). S. J. Ball's *The Cold War: An International History, 1947–1991* (New York: Arnold, 1998) is so far the best of several attempts to see the Cold War in broader terms than simply a bipolar confrontation between the United States and the Soviet Union. A good account of the arms race is Ronald E. Powaski, *The Cold War: The United States and the Soviet Union, 1917–1991* (New York: Oxford University Press, 1998). See also Michael Kort, *The Columbia Guide to the Cold War* (New York: Columbia University Press, 1998), and the *Journal of Cold War Studies* (1999–).

Useful surveys of military technology are Robert L. O'Connell, *Of Arms and Men: A History of War, Weapons, and Aggression* (New York: Oxford University Press, 1989), and Martin L. Van Creveld, *Technology and War: From 2000 B.C. to the Present* (rev. and expanded ed., New York: Free Press, 1991). The critical issue of secrecy is best approached through Herbert N. Foerstel, *Secret Science: Federal Control of American Science and Technology* (Westport, Conn.: Praeger, 1993), and Harold Relyea, *Silencing Science: National Security Controls and Scientific Communication* (Norwood, N.J.: Ablex Pub., 1994). In a class by itself is John H. Perkins, *Geopolitics and the Green Revolution: Wheat, Genes, and the Cold War* (New York: Oxford University Press, 1997).

Samuel P. Huntington defines civil-military relations in his classic *The Soldier and the State: The Theory and Politics of Civil-Military Relations* (Cambridge, Mass.: Belknap Press of Harvard University Press, 1957). Morris Janowitz provides an antidote to Huntington's politics and ideology in *The Professional Soldier: A Social and Political Portrait* (Glencoe, Ill.: Free Press, 1960), but no work has superseded Huntington's conceptualization of the issue. Peter Feaver, author of *Guarding the Guardians: Civilian Control of Nuclear Weapons in the United States,* Cornell Studies in Security Affairs (Ithaca, N.Y.: Cornell University Press, 1992), takes on that challenge in his forthcoming *Armed Servants: Agency, Oversight, and Civil-Military Relations.* The defining case study of civil-military relations in the Cold War was the F-111, explored most cogently in Robert J. Art, *The TFX Decision: McNamara and the Military* (Boston: Little, Brown, 1968) and Robert F. Coulam, *Illusions of Choice: The F-111 and the Problem of Weapons Acquisition Reform* (Princeton, N.J.: Princeton University Press, 1977). Bureaucratic struggles such as this led Seymour Melman to believe that Robert McNamara had created a capitalist state.

The best of the Vietnam-era studies of abuses within the defense industry is still Harold L. Nieburg, *In the Name of Science* (rev. ed., Chicago: Quadrangle Books, 1970). Excellent case studies abound, such as Nick Kotz, *Wild Blue Yonder: Money, Politics, and the B-1 Bomber* (Princeton, N.J.: Princeton University Press, 1989), and Berkeley Rice, *The C-5A Scandal: An Inside Story of the Military-*

Industrial Complex (Boston: Houghton Mifflin, 1971), both drawn from the aerospace industry. David Noble applies Marxist categories of analysis to air force development of numerically controlled machine tools in *Forces of Production: A Social History of Industrial Automation* (New York: Knopf, 1984). The shifting demography of American industry is traced in Anne R. Markusen, *The Rise of the Gunbelt: The Remappping of Industrial America* (New York: Oxford University Press, 1991).

Ballistic missile development has proven to be a particularly fertile field in which to explore both the government-industry relationship and the interactions between agencies of the executive branch. Michael H. Armacost, in *The Politics of Weapons Innovation: The Thor-Jupiter Controversy* (New York: Columbia University Press, 1969), and Edmund Beard in *Developing the ICBM: A Study in Bureaucratic Politics* (New York: Columbia University Press, 1976), investigate the missile mess of the 1950s. Donald A. Mackenzie applies social constructivism to the relations between government and industry, as well as the relations between government agencies, in *Inventing Accuracy: An Historical Sociology of Nuclear Missile Guidance* (Cambridge, Mass.: MIT Press, 1990). Harvey M. Sapolsky reveals in *The Polaris System Development: Bureaucratic and Programmatic Success in Government* (Cambridge, Mass.: Harvard University Press, 1972) that the Program Evaluation and Review Technique developed to manage this complex project had more to do with public relations and mollification of Congress than with systems development. John Lonnquest comes to similar conclusions in his study of the Atlas missile program, "The Face of Atlas: General Bernard Schriever and The Development of the Atlas Intercontinental Ballistic Missile, 1953–1960," PhD dissertation, Duke University, 1996. George A. Reed's analysis of the Minuteman program ("U.S. Defense Policy, U.S. Air Force Doctrine, and Strategic Nuclear Weapon Systems, 1958–1964: The Case of the Minuteman ICBM," PhD dissertation, Duke University, 1986) suggests that the navy and the air force worried more about each other than they did about the Soviet Union.

The scientific and technical communities enjoyed their greatest power and influence in the Eisenhower administration. In addition to Kistiakowsky's *A Scientist at the White House*, see the account of his predecessor as Eisenhower's science advisor, James R. Killian, *Sputnik, Scientists, and Eisenhower: A Memoir of the First Special Assistant to the President for Science and Technology* (Cambridge, Mass.: MIT Press, 1977). An informed and insightful overview of science advice to the president appears in Gregg Herken, *Cardinal Choices: Presidential Science Advising from the Atomic Bomb to SDI* (New York: Oxford University Press, 1992). Dissent over the Vietnam War undermined relations between the scientific community and Presidents Johnson and Nixon; by the end of Nixon's tenure the golden age of science advice to the president, based in part on the stature of physicists following World War II, had come to an end. For different views of this critical phenomenon, see Daniel J. Kevles, *The Physicists: The History of a Scientific Community in Modern America* (New York: Knopf, distributed by Random House, 1978); Daniel Lee Kleinman, *Politics on the Endless Frontier: Postwar Research Policy in the United States* (Durham, N.C.: Duke University Press, 1995); and Jessica Lang, *American Science in an Age of Anxiety: Scientists, Anticommunism, and the Cold War* (Chapel Hill: University of North Carolina Press, 1999).

The salience of the military-industrial complex peaked at just the moment when the Western world grew most alarmed about technological determinism. The essential starting point is Langdon Winner, *Autonomous Technology: Technics Out of Control As a Theme in Political Thought* (Cambridge, Mass.: MIT Press, 1977). It should be read in conjunction with two alarmist tracts of the 1960s, Jacques Ellul, *The Technological Society* (New York: Vintage Books, 1964), and Lewis Mumford, *The Myth of the Machine,* 2 vols. (New York: Harcourt, Brace & World, 1967–70), esp. vol. 1, *The Pentagon of Power.* Jonathan Schell captures the public's very real fear that nuclear weapons were an autonomous technology that would soon determine *The Fate of the Earth* (New York: Knopf, 1982). Spencer Weart traces the spread of that apprehension into daily life in *Nuclear Fear: A History of Images* (Cambridge, Mass.: Harvard University Press, 1988), while Sheldon Ungar, in *The Rise and Fall of Nuclearism: Fear and Faith as Determinants of the Arms Race* (University Park, Pa.: Pennsylvania State University Press, 1992), explores its effect on the arms race itself. Laura Elizabeth Hein and Mark Selden compare two different national manifestations of this phenomenon in *Living with the Bomb: American and Japanese Cultural Conflicts in the Nuclear Age* (Armonk, N.Y.: M. E. Sharpe, 1997). Other useful studies of the American experience include Margot Henriksen, *Dr. Strangelove's America: Society and Culture in the Atomic Age* (Berkeley: University of California Press, 1997), and Fred Inglis, *The Cruel Peace: Everyday Life in the Cold War* (New York: Basic Books, 1991).